imaginations:

MORE THAN YOU THINK

OTHER BOOKS BY JAMES P. GILLS, M.D.

(with HeartLight)
The Unseen Essential: A Story for Our Troubled Times (ISBN 1-879938-05-7)
A compelling, contemporary novel about one man's
struggle to grow into God's kind of love.

Love: Fulfilling the Ultimate Quest (ISBN 1-879938-02-2)
A quick refresher course on the meaning and method
of God's great gift.

The Dynamics of Worship (ISBN 1-879938-03-0)
Designed to rekindle the heart with a passionate love for God.
Gives the who, what, when, where, why and how of worship.

Temple Maintenance: Excellence With Love (ISBN 1-879938-01-4)
A how-to book for achieving lifelong total fitness of body,
mind and spirit.

Come Unto Me (ISBN 1-879938-00-6)
Explores God's eternal desire for mankind to know
Him intimately.

Tender Journey (ISBN 1-879938-17-0)
The sequel to The Unseen Essential, a story of love
and family.

(With Victoria Krueger)
**The Prayerful Spirit: Passion for God,
Compassion for People** (ISBN 1-879938-10-3)
Tells how prayer has changed Dr. Gills' life, the lives of his
patients and the lives of other doctors. (With Victoria Krueger
and Kathy Saunders)

Believe and Rejoice! (ISBN 1-879938-13-7)
Explores how faith in God can fill our lives with His joy.

Rx for Worry: A Thankful Heart (ISBN 1-879938-14-6)
Discusses how each of us can find peace by resting
and relaxing in the promises of God.

imaginations:

MORE THAN YOU THINK

BY JAMES P. GILLS, M.D.

With Victoria C. Krueger

Published by LOVE PRESS
A Ministry of St. Luke's Cataract and Laser Institute
2000

Imaginations: More Than You Think
© 2000 by James P. Gills, M.D.
ISBN 1-879938-18-9

Published by Love Press
An international outreach of St. Luke's Cataract & Laser Institute
Tarpon Springs, Florida
Printed in the United States of America
First printing: 100,000
Second printing: 100,000

Cover and book design by Joanne Smout and Aaron Grudis
Cover art by Mark Erickson

For information, contact Love Press
43309 U.S. 19 N, P.O. Box 5000, Tarpon Springs, FL 34688-5000
Telephone (727) 938-2020, Ext. 2200, (800) 282-9905, Ext. 2200
www.lovepress.com

DEDICATION

This book is dedicated to all those who seek to turn their minds and hearts closer to God. May each of us follow in the footsteps of Jonathan Edwards, aligning ourselves with God and finding perfect joy and satisfaction in His thoughts.

Table of Contents

ACKNOWLEDGMENTS

This book would not have been possible without the contributions and support of many people. First, let me thank my good friend and colleague, Gary Carter. Gary's insight and wisdom have guided countless discussions about how we can focus our minds on Christ and the rich blessings we receive from Him.

I am also deeply grateful to the many staff members at St. Luke's who have been partners in prayer and praise throughout the writing of this book. I want to extend a special thanks to Lois Babcock for her support and timely words of encouragement. And to the patients at St. Luke's, let me say thank you for all the examples of faith and focus you have shown.

The contributions of my wife, Heather, have been invaluable. Her love, rooted in the love of God, continues to be a source of inspiration to me.

INTRODUCTION

DURING THE WRITING OF THIS BOOK, I HAD A LOT ON MY MIND—THOUGHTS I REALLY NEEDED TO CLEAN UP. MY HEAD WAS A BIT "OFF KILTER" BECAUSE I HAD BEEN INJURED, FIRST IN A BIKING ACCIDENT, THEN IN A SKIING ACCIDENT.

I certainly was able to continue practicing medicine, but I wasn't able to do the long-distance athletics that always had been such a big part of my life. I couldn't run or bike or windsurf—all those fun activities I had enjoyed during my after-work hours.

I tried to find other forms of entertainment, but nothing quite fit the bill. My lifestyle and my self-image had changed dramatically, and I wasn't content.

With so much change in my physical abilities, I decided to go back to something I had done earlier in my life— trading on the stock market. Lo and behold! I made much more money in the market than I did in medicine! Having been trained in the very astute discipline of the psychology of trading, I actually fared better than the managed funds did (with the exception of Internet funds).

However, I became so intense with my trading that it actually started to consume my life. My mind was always filled with the stock market! It was taking time away from my wife, my family and my friends. More importantly, it was taking away from my time with the Lord.

I realized there was a major difference in my mindset on the days I read the newspaper and neglected the Scriptures. I was not at peace. I did not have deep inner joy. Instead, I was preoccupied with the market and my success. Even though I stood to gain very little because most of the profits were for charity, the thrill of winning had me hooked! When I realized I was reading the *Investor's Business Daily* newspaper more than I was reading my Bible, I knew I had to get my perspective back.

In the Christian life, some lessons are learned again and again. The lesson brought home to me during this time is that *what we think is what we become.*

As I studied the newspaper more and the Bible less, I became weaker in the Word. When any of us are weak in the Word, our thoughts are open to the assaults of the world—the temptations and lures of sin. And because our thoughts run our life, we must constantly guard them so they don't lead us into a life of sin.

A little sleep, a little slumber, a little folding of the hands to rest — and poverty will come on you like a bandit and scarcity like an armed man.
Proverbs 24:33-34

The writer of Proverbs makes clear that we won't fall into the deep pits of sin overnight. It's a gradual process. We begin to rest and become complacent in our faith journey. We don't guard our thoughts and actions with diligence. Therefore, our thoughts focus increasingly on worldly matters and focus less on godly ones. Those small steps we take as we rest eventually have huge consequences. It's essential that we constantly guard our thoughts and our actions, or we will fall victim to sin.

Thankfully, God wakes us up and intervenes. He shows us where we're stepping out of the path and, as a faithful Shepherd to our soul, brings us back to the cross. He is the living God! He shows us, again and again, that we are saved only through His grace.

I was challenged by the Word of God. Because I was on crutches for a good part of two years, I could no longer focus on long-distance athletics. My head was filled first with thoughts of the stock market. But it didn't take long for me to learn there was no true life there. And I understood anew the impact of my thoughts on my life.

We are foolish when we give ourselves over to the thought patterns of the world and turn our backs on the Lord and His glory! Ungodly thoughts will be followed by ungodly actions that will draw us farther away from God.

My prayer, and the purpose of this book, is that each of us will understand how rich our life is when we focus our thoughts on God. **Explore with me three basic concepts:**

- We are what we think. Our thoughts determine our actions.

- God is most glorified in us when we are most satisfied in Him. Our greatest joy is surrendering our thoughts, and our life, to God.

- Our thoughts now affect how we'll spend eternity. When our thoughts are faithfully focused on God, we'll be rewarded with an eternal mindset. We'll have a glimpse of eternity now, and we'll be richly rewarded in His presence in heaven.

Our thoughts must be filled with all the fullness of God. Then we will see His glory, His wonder, His beauty and His worth. He will be our complete and perfect joy now and for eternity. Amen and Amen!

We are What We Think

Let me ask it this way. Are our thoughts important? Does it matter what we think?

"Be careful what you think because
your thoughts run your life."

That's the New Century Version of Proverbs 4:23. I think that verse sums it up pretty well. For each of us, what we think is truly who we are. Whether we're tall or short, rich or poor, black or white, male or female, young or old, our thoughts and imaginations determine who we are and what we do.

In many areas we rely on what I call our "imaginations of the mind." Imagination is an ability God has given us that can be used for our good or for our harm. We might define imagination as "the image-making faculty of the mind."

The imagination molds our mind, our thoughts, our ideas and our attitudes. Imaginations become a pattern of thinking and a whole mindset toward life that determines our creativity, our emotions, our outlook, our self-discipline, our ability to solve problems and our ability to handle the choices we make every day.

Albert Einstein said that "Imagination is more important than knowledge." That's because all our imaginations affect us. They either help us or hurt us. And it's up to us how we choose to use them.

Athletes, for example, use their imaginations as part of their training regimen. Vicki Huber, an Olympic runner, says she creates a mental picture of her race before it begins. She imagines all the possible situations that might occur during the race. "And I always picture myself winning," Huber says.

Most important, our imaginations bring us to God as He calls us to "come unto me."

In the Old Testament, two primary words are used to translate the word "imaginations." Each is used in both a positive and a negative manner, showing the positive and negative power of imaginations.

> O Lord, God of our fathers Abraham, Isaac and Israel, keep this desire [imaginations] in the hearts of your people forever, and keep their hearts loyal to you.
> **I Chronicles 29:18**

The word used here is the Hebrew word *Yetser* (Hebrew listing number 3336 in *The New Strong's Exhaustive Concordance of the Bible)*. King David had dedicated all the materials for the temple. He offered this beautiful prayer of God's greatness and glory and power, charging Solomon to keep God's people faithful in their thoughts of the Lord.

On this wonderful day in God's presence, David prayed for God to continually keep this day in the imaginations of the hearts of His people. He sought for their minds to be filled with imaginations that were holy and godly.

Here's a negative use of the word *Yetser*:

> The Lord saw how great man's wickedness on the earth had become, and that every inclination [imagination] of the thoughts of his heart was only evil all the time.
> **Genesis 6:5**

In this verse, *Yetser* means the imaginations of man's heart were continually evil, and they were the reason God sent the flood.

The second word is *hagah* (Hebrew listing number 1897 in *The New Strong's Exhaustive Concordance of the Bible*).

> But his delight is in the law of the Lord, and on his law he meditates [imagines] day and night.
> **Psalm 1:2**

> Do not let this Book of the Law depart from your mouth; meditate on it day and night, so that you may be careful to do everything written in it.
> **Joshua 1:8**

Our meditations, our imagination, should be filled with the Word of God. These verses stress that all our meditations should be focused on God. It is not an exercise to be taken lightly, but it should be done diligently and continually.

Look at the negative use:

> Why do the nations conspire and the peoples plot [imagine] in vain?
> **Psalm 2:1**

Hagah describes nations imagining how to get rid of God's commands and their responsibility to Him. Their meditations are not focused on the Lord. They are full of rebellion, selfishness and conceit. And, in the end, all their efforts will be in vain. They will not succeed. The Lord will always be victorious. And He will guide us when our thoughts are headed in the right direction.

The Apostle Paul tells us where we should direct our thoughts:

> Finally, brothers, whatever is true, whatever is noble, whatever is right, whatever is pure, whatever is lovely, whatever is admirable—if anything is excellent or praiseworthy— think about such things.
> **Philippians 4:8**

The true, the noble, the right, the pure, the lovely, the admirable, the excellent, the praiseworthy: These are godly imaginations. When we're filled with these holy imaginations, our actions will honor and glorify God.

Think of it as a clock. Our priorities are the hour hands. They set the general direction of our life. Our thoughts and imaginations are the minute and second hands. They give us our energy and our vision.

Our attitudes, our inner imaginations, our inner state of peace or anxiety, determine our actions. Our actions and our words show what we really are inside.

Jesus knew this when He criticized the Pharisees:

> Woe to you, teachers of the law and Pharisees, you hypocrites! You clean the outside of the cup and dish, but inside they are full of greed and self-indulgence. Blind Pharisee! First clean the inside of the cup and dish, and then the outside also will be clean.
> **Matthew 23:25-26**

The inside of the cup, our mindset, is what's important. Our imaginations determine our actions. Jesus says it bluntly:

> For out of the heart come evil thoughts, murder, adultery, sexual immorality, theft, false testimony, slander.
> **Matthew 15:19**

We will fall, we will fail, if we let the wrong thoughts direct our actions. We must open our mind and heart to the true imaginations of life—God and His eternal promises.

Most important, our fate for eternity hangs in the balance of what we're thinking today. Our thought patterns for this life will mold our life for eternity. We will be rewarded for our faithfulness when we keep our thoughts focused on Him.

What God really wants is for our inner life to be directed toward Him! He doesn't care for outward display or shows—what we wear, our skin color, our appearance, our height, our bank balance. He cares about our thoughts and how they direct our actions, now and for eternity.

The foundation of life—for all the details of life, and for all of our life's endeavors—is that we are focused on Him, and that our thoughts remain faithful to Him now and, consequently, for eternity. The secret to our daily life is to turn all of our thoughts to Him so that our most important imagination is to always think of Him.

Searching for Satisfaction

LET'S GO BACK TO THAT RECORDING OF YOUR THOUGHTS WE DISCUSSED IN THE PREVIOUS CHAPTER. WHAT WERE YOU THINKING ABOUT? WERE YOU THINKING ABOUT WHETHER YOU HAVE WHAT YOU WANT—ENOUGH MONEY, ENOUGH SUCCESS, ENOUGH TIME? WERE YOU THINKING ABOUT WHETHER YOU ARE HAPPY? DO YOU FEEL FULFILLED OR DO YOU FEEL THAT SOMETHING IS MISSING?

This is a question that goes back to the beginning of humanity. Adam and Eve had everything they could ever want in the Garden of Eden. Yet they wanted more. And Satan knew how to use that imagination—that desire for wanting more—to lure them away from focusing on God first.

> "For God knows that when you eat [the fruit from the tree] your eyes will be opened, and you will be like God, knowing good and evil."
> **Genesis 3:5**

So Eve, and then Adam, ate the fruit. The result? They were banished from the Garden of Eden, where everything had been given to them, and sent to work the land for themselves. The seeds for each of our struggles with choosing between God and worldly desires were sown with the actions of Adam and Eve.

I know people, and I'm sure you do too, who are always searching for satisfaction. Some imagine they will find satisfaction in their work, so they go from job to job, never finding the perfect fit. Others think satisfaction is found in what they can get out of a relationship with another person. So these folks drift from relationship to relationship, unable to give of themselves and never receiving very much. Still others settle for fleeting sensual pleasures rather than lasting satisfaction. They end up abusing alcohol or drugs. Sometimes they see life as a series of meaningless sexual encounters. Some desire so much what others have that they steal, or even kill, to get what they want.

Why do people do this?

The analyst Sigmund Freud spent a lot of years observing human thought and behavior. His conclusion was that it's just our nature. No matter what we have, it's not enough. People are never satisfied because they are selfish; they always want more.

He thought our condition was hopeless.

But that's not what God thinks!

God has created all of us with the desire for true contentment. We all have a void in our heart that yearns to be filled. We may seek all kinds of activities and relationships to find satisfaction. But God knows nothing the world offers will ever satisfy us. According to worldly standards, we will never have enough money, enough fame, enough success or enough love.

That's why God did something that has changed my life and can change your life! He sent His son, Jesus Christ, to die on a cross and rise from the dead. He let His son die so that we could live. He sent His son as a sacrifice so you and I could have eternal life. He made right the relationship that Adam and Eve had broken.

> Very rarely will anyone die for a righteous man, though for a good man someone might possibly dare to die. But God demonstrates his own love for us in this: While we were still sinners, Christ died for us.
> **Romans 5:7-8**

Now, Sigmund Freud didn't understand this. It doesn't make sense that someone would give up his life for another.

But Jesus took normal human attitudes and turned them upside down. He tells us that what the world offers us—our money, our jobs, our activities, our relationships—isn't important. There's something completely new that will give us total satisfaction: focusing on the mind of Christ.

> The man without the Spirit does not accept the things that come from the Spirit of God, for they are foolishness to him, and he cannot understand them, because they are spiritually discerned. The spiritual man makes judgments about all things, but he himself is not subject to man's judgment:
>
> "For who has known the mind of the Lord that he may instruct him?" But we have the mind of Christ.
> **I Corinthians 2:14-16**

Our sense of satisfaction in Christ will never make sense to those focused on worldly desires. Our union with the mind of Christ will appear foolish to the world. But it doesn't matter. We have surrendered to the pure and perfect love of Jesus Christ! We have imaginations centered on Christ!

Each of us can feel, deep in our soul, how powerful it is to have our thoughts and imaginations filled with, engulfed in and focused on the living God. We can feel the new life that comes from faith flowing through us, enveloping us, guiding us and healing us. We are united with Christ. He lives in us!

Freud and Christ are at opposite ends of the spectrum of imaginations: total selfishness and total satisfaction.

Total selfishness is insatiable desire. This is more than normal desires and a healthy lifestyle. It's total uneasiness and unrest. It's neurosis, where we still function in society, but not very well. And it's psychosis, where we're no longer able to function—we steal, we abuse verbally or physically, we kill. Selfishness is a cascade of desires that are never filled.

The opposite of total selfishness is total satisfaction. Total satisfaction is to be found only in Jesus Christ. Our wants are never filled until they're filled by Christ. God created us for this purpose—to find our full satisfaction in Him. Author John Piper says it this way: God is most glorified in us when we are most satisfied in Him. We find true contentment when we believe the promises of God and accept the eternal life He has given us through Jesus Christ.

The search for satisfaction is part of the human condition. Many people seek satisfaction through imaginations that are not of God. They have imaginations of worldly power, sex, money, popularity and success.

But we can only be truly and completely satisfied through Jesus Christ! God gives us perfect joy and peace when we choose to think about Him and fill our minds with godly thoughts.

A pastor I know tells a story about a king who was very upset. He went to the court magician to ask how he could find contentment. The magician said the king needed to find the shirt of a man who is truly content and to wear that shirt day and night for a month.

So the king sent his men to search throughout the kingdom to find such a man. It took months before they finally returned. They reported to the king that they had found only one content man. The king stormed around and demanded, "Well, where's the shirt? Don't keep me waiting!"

The men paused and then said, "The man who was truly content had no shirt."

Contentment can never be found in possessions, in success, in a career, in physical achievements. The king who looked for contentment had everything but contentment because he was looking in the wrong place. Contentment never comes from external sources. It can only be found through the imagination of knowing Christ will meet all our needs.

Psalm 23:1 says, "I shall not be in want." God is our portion; He will provide for us. All we need is to be near Him and walk with Him.

That imagination, that faith in Jesus Christ, has changed my life! Hear how it changed someone else:

> I have learned to be content whatever the circumstances. I know what it is to be in need, and I know what it is to have plenty. I have learned the secret of being content in any and every situation, whether well fed or hungry, whether living

in plenty or in want. I can do everything through
him who gives me strength.
Philippians 4:11-13

The Apostle Paul wrote this while he was sitting in
a Roman prison. He didn't know how long he would be there.
He didn't even know whether he would survive or be put
to death.

But it didn't matter because Paul knew the key to true
contentment: He knew this Jesus who had died on the cross
for him. He knew this Jesus who rose from the dead for him.
He knew this Savior who walked with him every day through
the power of the Holy Spirit. He knew this Jesus who has
given him a home in heaven!

Paul had faith in God's eternal promise that He would
provide. Paul knew, in his head and in his heart, that God
would give him strength to meet all his needs. And he could
rejoice, regardless of his external circumstances, because he
had faith in God's provision not just for a moment, but for all
eternity. That faith is what filled Paul, and what can fill each
of us, with God's perfect peace and satisfaction.

Jesus did that for Paul, and He provides it for you and for
me! We can walk with Him, we can talk with Him, we can feel
His presence every day. Now and for eternity.

This imagination gives each of us a totally new perspective. Money, fame and success don't matter. We don't want,
and we certainly don't need, what this world offers. Those are
no longer important. We see what's truly important—a personal relationship with God through Jesus Christ that lasts
now and for all of eternity!

Sadly, we live in a world filled with evil, earthly philoso-
phies. We're barraged with a constant flow of worldly concepts through television, radio, newspapers, magazines,
books and the Internet.

That's why the words of Paul are so important. They
remind us that we have eternal life! What can Madison
Avenue advertising offer to compete? We no longer have the
mind of the world. We are no longer lured away by the lies of
the world, which ensnare us.

Genuine contentment in life is found only in the deep, permanent and beautiful mindset of Christ Jesus. Actions guided by His wisdom, with faith in His promises, produce that sense of satisfaction.

> My soul will be satisfied as with the richest of foods;
> with singing lips my mouth will praise you.
> **Psalm 63:5**

This God-centered attitude can change your life! When we find satisfaction in the eternal promises of God we're filled with peace and joy, patience and thanksgiving. We're no longer selfish. We're satisfied with God's eternal provision.

Worry and fear are gone! Bitterness and anger have been replaced with forgiveness and love. We are confident that He will provide for each of us now and for eternity because He has promised He would.

> Come, all you who are thirsty,
> come to the waters;
> and you who have no money,
> come, buy and eat!
> Come, buy wine and milk
> without money and without cost.
> Why spend money on what is not bread,
> and your labor on what does not satisfy?
> Listen, listen to me, and eat what is good,
> and your soul will delight in the richest of fare.
> **Isaiah 55:1-2**

This is a tremendous Gospel offer! "Come to the Lord. Let Him provide. This is what will help you." Here is the energetic call of the Almighty God welcoming the dissatisfied heart to come to Him for true satisfaction.

Only in God's free grace can we find satisfaction. Otherwise, we labor for that which does not satisfy us. We are concerned with outward appearances. We are absorbed with our own importance and the impressions we make on others.

We are consumed with the physical life rather than the inner life. We exhaust ourselves searching for external satisfaction.

Sometimes we get so focused on details that we lose sight of the overall picture. May the words of Paul encourage us:

> Therefore we do not lose heart. Though outwardly we are wasting away, yet inwardly we are being renewed day by day. For our light and momentary troubles are achieving for us an eternal glory that far outweighs them all. So we fix our eyes not on what is seen, but on what is unseen. For what is seen is temporary, but what is unseen is eternal.
> **II Corinthians 4:16-18**

The world tells us material goods and measures of success are important. The Bible tells us what's really important are the eternal priorities of God. What we can see is temporary; it doesn't last. We need to put our hope in the invisible and the eternal promises of God.

Focusing on our eternal relationship with Him changes our daily behavior. Earthly measures of success are not important because we are in an eternal relationship with Him. With an eternal perspective, we realize we don't need to be successful in other people's eyes. We don't need to try to live up to their expectations.

We have everything and are everything in Christ! The possessions we have mean nothing. We don't need to worry and fret about matters that aren't important for very long. Our afflictions are nothing compared to the eternal joy and eternal glory we're going to receive in Christ Jesus.

Most important, we are transformed! There's a Greek word for this transformation: *metanoia*. *Meta* means change, *noia* means thoughts. We are changing our thoughts and focusing on God. A basic concept of salvation is having a God-centered attitude. With *metanoia*, we see how God's grace wipes away our old ways of thinking, our old imaginations. We see what's truly important. We are His children, and we are engulfed in His love.

We can't be the same after we have had this transformation—this *metanoia*. Our thoughts and actions are different because we are anchored in God. We are rooted in Him. We are satisfied with Him and Him alone.

Let's examine the words of Paul again.

I have learned to be content whatever the circumstances. I know what it is to be in need, and I know what it is to have plenty. I have learned the secret of being content in any and every situation, whether well fed or hungry, whether living in plenty or in want. I can do everything through him who gives me strength.
Philippians 4:11-13

Knowing how to be content when we're in want requires an extra measure of diligence. All of us struggle at times with wanting more, or with comparing what we have with others. Remember the secret that Paul shares with us. We can do everything through Christ. We don't have to possess more than we have now, or possess more than other people. We need nothing more to satisfy us than our imaginations of Christ.

It's just as important that we stay focused on Christ when we are "well-fed." Being content when we're prosperous means we are still content in God's provision for our life. We still don't seek more. And we give God the glory for what He has provided. We're not proud of having so much, because we know God has given it to us. We don't claim to have achieved it by ourselves.

We must remember that He is all we should want and, in an active sense, He is all we do want. He will always satisfy us! He will always fill us! He is all-sufficient, now and for eternity!

Then we can grow in our satisfaction in Jesus Christ and become faithful followers through His grace. We become intimate with Jesus, we commit our lives to Him, and we seek to let His mind and His thoughts be ours.

Why is growing in Christ so important? Because our thoughts today affect our future and shape who we will be for eternity!

Imaginations focused on Christ allow us to feel God's presence in all circumstances. They allow us to reach up and see eternity! These imaginations allow us to see God's vision of life for us, because our heart is melted with God in eternity.

We need to imagine ourselves eternally with God. We need to imagine the Holy Spirit always with us. We need to incline our heart toward Him. When we come to the Lord, we are content in Him. We find satisfaction because we know what we have right now is sufficient because of His generous gift. We need to seek nothing else.

Faith is being satisfied with our relationship with the Lord through Jesus Christ. We aren't distracted by the world when we're satisfied in His promises. When our minds are fixed on Him, we are weaned away from our earthly focus. We're faithfully and fervently focused on Christ, our love for Him and our commitment to Him.

Let us turn our eyes, our heart and our mind to Jesus and the transforming power of His death and glorious resurrection. We find perfect peace and joy when we are engulfed in our Creator, Redeemer and Sustainer, the one who liberates us from the selfishness that leads to sin and death. In God, through Christ Jesus, we find eternal satisfaction, eternal love and eternal life. Let us turn our mind to seeking complete satisfaction in Him!

Fixing Our Eyes on Jesus

A LIFE FILLED WITH SATISFIED IMAGINATIONS IS GLORIOUS! THOSE IMAGINATIONS CAN CAPTIVATE US WITH GOD. WE WANT TO EMBRACE GOD. WE KNOW, IN OUR HEAD AND IN OUR HEART, THAT HIS PROMISES TO US ARE REAL. THESE IMAGINATIONS BRING US A GENUINE SENSE OF SATISFACTION AND JOY IN THE LIFE GOD HAS GIVEN US.

But what happens when worldly thoughts sneak in? Do they really affect our lives—and our actions?

Remember, our thoughts direct our actions. We are what we think. If we think selfishly, we will be selfish. And when we're selfish, we're not satisfied with Christ. We're not filled with imaginations of an eternal relationship with Him. Our thoughts every day affect our life for eternity.

The test for whether the imaginations of our daily life will help us or hurt us is simple: Do they reflect the mind of Christ? Paul emphasizes in his letter to the Philippians that the foundation for a peaceful, joyful, godly life is godly thinking. Let's look again at his instruction.

> Finally, brothers, whatever is true, whatever is noble, whatever is right, whatever is pure, whatever is lovely, whatever is admirable—if anything is excellent or praiseworthy—think about such things.
> **Philippians 4:8**

The best way to get rid of a bad habit is to replace it with a good one. The essential ingredient to replace selfish imaginations is Jesus Christ.

Struggles with the lures of this world are displaced in our mind as we think on our Lord, Jesus Christ. He will help us guide our imaginations.

Then we'll wake up in the morning full of thanksgiving and joy and love. We'll be upright in rejoicing, rather than beaten down in cynicism. We'll be conquerors for God, not conquered by the world.

> Let us fix our eyes on Jesus, the author and perfecter of our faith, who for the joy set before him endured the cross, scorning its shame, and sat down at the right hand of the throne of God. Consider him who endured such opposition from sinful men, so that you will not grow weary and lose heart.
> **Hebrews 12:2-3**

The person of Jesus Christ should always be before us and incorporated within us. We need to make sure we think of Jesus and start out the day with Him, and then be conscious of Him throughout the day.

A story about Mother Teresa illustrates this point. A group of people had been with her for a while and asked what they could pray about for her. She replied: "Pray that I will never get so involved in Jesus' work that I forget Jesus." She wanted to make sure that she was thinking first of Jesus in whatever she did. She didn't want the zeal for her work to replace her zeal for Christ.

Now we all have thoughts and desires. The outcome, though, depends on whether we are satisfied in God's promises or whether we covet the material goods of this world. We will either live in a great jail of the mind or we will live a life engulfed with God.

When we're satisfied, our thoughts are focused on God. We're filled with faith, peace and love because we know He is providing all we need.

At the other end of the spectrum is a life of sin dictated by insatiable want. All the sin in our life stems from failing to believe God will provide. I'd like to call it the "psychosis of wanting." We're selfish. We will destroy ourselves and those around us because we no longer have faith in the promises of God.

> Like a city whose walls are broken down is a man who lacks self-control.
> **Proverbs 25:28**

God's Word is clear on this point: We need to control our thoughts or they will destroy us.

For example, there's a difference between sexual desire and lust. Desire is normal and healthy. It lets us share our love with our spouse. It enables us to have children. It lets us be male or female. But lust is desire gone awry. It's a focus on the world that goes beyond what God says is good and right for us. Unchecked desire can destroy us.

The unchecked desire, or lust, for any of the things of this world isolates us from God and will destroy us. These "vain imaginations" can include our occupation, possessions, social status, sports, sensual interests or anything else that can fill our mind and become an obsession. We are so easily fooled by the wrong things. We need to have Jesus before us at all times.

> No temptation has seized you except what is common to man. And God is faithful; he will not let you be tempted beyond what you can bear. But when you are tempted, he will also provide a way out so that you can stand up under it.
> **1 Corinthians 10:13**

There are no new or original temptations. God has seen them all. He has seen many people in the same struggles we face every day. And God loves us so much, and so faithfully, that He will provide in those moments of greatest weakness. He will throw us the lifeline. But it's up to us to grab it.

We don't have the strength within ourselves alone to overcome temptation. That's why we're told in Ephesians 6:10 to "be strong in the Lord and in his mighty power."

We cannot change our thoughts by our own power. The only power we have is to submit and surrender to God. Through His sovereignty and power, then, we are able to overcome the imaginations of the world, the evil that comes from Satan, the sin that comes from unbelief. We need to accept the Lord, find our strength in Him, and then we will overcome.

How do we respond to the constant battle between our faith in God's promises and our desire for worldly possessions and worldly acceptance? We need to return to God's Word to remember His promises.

> Whom have I in heaven but you?
> And earth has nothing I desire besides you.
> **Psalm 73:25**

Do we desire what the world offers or the rich blessings of God? Every day we must choose whether we focus on our personal relationship with Jesus Christ. Every day we must decide whether we're directed to the Lord or to Satan. It's important that we have a constant desire to be renewed day by day. Then we can get rid of the bondage that inhibits our life and get rid of the thoughts we know are wrong.

We react to the events of each day not because of a set of codes or rules, but because of our personal relationship with Him. This is not a strange enigma or mystery. It's an absolute truth of focus. When we re-pattern our thought processes to be Christ-like, we will have the joy of a Christ-filled life.

Faith in Action

WE KNOW WE'RE SUPPOSED TO FOCUS OUR THOUGHTS ON JESUS. BUT HOW DOES THIS APPLY TO OUR DAILY LIFE? JESUS TELLS US TO IMAGINE BUILDING A HOUSE:

> Therefore everyone who hears these words of mine and puts them into practice is like a wise man who built his house on the rock. The rain came down, the streams rose, and the winds blew and beat against that house; yet it did not fall, because it had its foundation on the rock.
> **Matthew 7:24-25**

What happens if we don't put His words into practice? Jesus warns us of the consequences:

> But everyone who hears these words of mine and does not put them into practice is like a foolish man who built his house on sand. The rain came down, the streams rose, and the winds blew and beat against that house, and it fell with a great crash.
> **Matthew 7:26-27**

Focusing our thoughts and then letting godly actions spring from those thoughts is the essence of our life. Our thoughts and actions must be aligned. We can't think one way and act another or we will end up torn apart. But when our thoughts and actions work together, our faith and experience turn hope into God's manifest reality. Our worldly desires are destroyed!

This is an important step to take as believers. When our thoughts and actions work together we can see evidence of our growing spiritual maturity. God wants us to grow. He has bestowed His gifts to us for that purpose:

> To prepare God's people for works of service, so that the body of Christ may be built up until we all reach unity in the faith and in the knowledge of the Son of God and become mature, attaining to the whole measure of the fullness of Christ.
> **Ephesians 4:12-13**

A mature faith is where we experience the fullness of Christ. Our desire to be filled with His fullness increases daily as we grow to see God's glory, His wonder, His beauty and His worth. When we mature, our thoughts and actions spring forth from the fullness of Christ, and we allow Him to be our joy and our portion. Our imaginations are integrated with Him.

Therefore, we must mature spiritually just as we mature physically and emotionally. In order to mature physically, we need nutrition and conditioning. Maturing spiritually is no different. Nutrition comes from the Word of God. Conditioning comes from aligning our thoughts and actions with His will.

> Anyone who lives on milk, being still an infant, is not acquainted with the teaching about righteousness.
> But solid food is for the mature, who by constant use have trained themselves to distinguish good from evil.
> Therefore let us leave the elementary teachings about Christ and go on to maturity.
> **Hebrews 5:13-6:1**

How do we know that we are maturing in Christ? Hear the warning written by James:

> Do not merely listen to the word, and so deceive yourselves. Do what it says.
> **James 1:22**

James tells us we must act out our faith or our faith is without maturity. We are mature when our house is built on the foundation of the Word and our actions flow from that foundation.

We also need to examine the motives behind our actions. Are our actions guided by Christ or by selfish desires?

> If anyone serves, he should do it with the strength God provides, so that in all things God may be praised through Jesus Christ.
> **I Peter 4:11**

Our actions must be guided by God through the Holy Spirit. Imagine a cup in a bucket of water. The cup is not only filled with water, it's surrounded by water. That's a picture of how the Spirit should direct us—the Holy Spirit filling us and surrounding us.

Let me tell you a story about a man who wanted to design a boat. He didn't want to build the *Titanic*, mind you, just a simple sailboat. Yet he wanted this sailboat to be one of the prettiest in the world. So he set to work on his dream. He did everything possible to make beautiful the parts of the boat that were above the water—the part of the boat that people could see. But underneath, he cut corners. When the engineer suggested a certain amount of weight be applied to the very lowest part of the keel, he ignored the advice. "Oh, nobody will see that part of the boat." So he used less weight to cut his costs.

Finally the day came to put the boat in the water. He brought all of his friends out to the pier to watch the launching of his boat. Everyone was awed at the boat's majestic appearance. But when the boat got out in the water, the heavy wind capsized it.

This boat owner chose to see the world in one way— giving priority to the visible appearance. His internal focus was off.

As Christians, it's essential we have the right focus. We can't merely act with the visible behavior appropriate for a Christian. We need to be guided in our actions by our foundation of faith in God's eternal promises.

For it is we who are the circumcision, we who worship by the Spirit of God, who glory in Christ Jesus, and who put no confidence in the flesh.
Philippians 3:3

Paul is warning his readers about putting too much stock in good works and external symbols of faith—such as circumcision. He says the followers of Christ are the "circumcision," meaning their heart is focused in worship of the Lord. They rejoice in Jesus alone. There are no longer shadows; the substance has come. They have no confidence in rules and outward actions. Their confidence is rooted in the promises of God.

So do not throw away your confidence; it will be richly rewarded. You need to persevere so that when you have done the will of God, you will receive what he has promised.
Hebrews 10:35-36

God has promised that He will provide for us now and for eternity. When we are totally in love with Christ and are faithfully focused on Him, we will be blessed with riches beyond our wildest imaginations! Therefore, it's essential that each of us has a circumcision of the heart—that we are filled with God's Spirit. Then our actions flow from His will and we mature spiritually.

What are our imaginations? Is our thinking based on what's above the water line, or what is below? Actions based on external priorities show a lack of Christian growth. Only the internal, our relationship with God, lives forever!

Anticipating Eternity

THOUGHTS AND ACTIONS UNITED IN THE SPIRIT OF GOD SHOW OUR GROWTH AS CHRISTIANS. WHEN WE GROW, WE EXPERIENCE THE FULLNESS OF GOD, WHICH IS A JOY BEYOND DESCRIPTION. OUR ABILITY TO GROW IS LIMITED ONLY BY OUR ABILITY TO FOCUS OUR THOUGHTS ON GOD AND OUR ABILITY TO BE FAITHFUL TO HIM.

There's another reason we should focus and stay faithful: There is a direct connection between this life and eternity. How we focus our minds now will be reflected in our eternity.

For example, those who develop their musical capacity appreciate the varieties and intricacies of classical music. They have a deepened capacity and appreciation. Those who have not developed this capacity hear music, but do not experience as much beauty.

In the same way, some have suggested that believers who have developed a deeper capacity for God on earth will have a deeper joy and glory and wonder in heaven. What God bestows on us in heaven is related to the spiritual capacities we develop in this life. The way we live is the way we anticipate eternity.

God will preserve our mindset and our personality for eternity to the degree that we have become like Christ. He saves us by His grace, and He is going to preserve us, who were made by His Word for eternity.

In response to His grace, we are commanded to be faithful in our imaginations so we can constantly focus on Him.

> So then, men ought to regard us as servants of Christ and as those entrusted with the secret things of God. Now it is required that those who have been given a trust must prove faithful.
> **I Corinthians 4:1-2**

God's Word tells us we will be rewarded for being faithful, in thoughts and actions, to His Word and His promises.

> Whatever you do, work at it with all your heart, as working for the Lord, not for men, since you know that you will receive an inheritance from the Lord as a reward.
> **Colossians 3:23-24**

God rewards each of us for being faithful to Him—in our thoughts and actions. Faithfulness is not merely external. It is not just how faithful we seem in our actions—going to church, donating time or money. Our thoughts need to be faithful to Him as well. Through our faithfulness in thought and action, we are thankful, we are surrendered and we are abandoned to Him. Our faithfulness to Him determines our eternal reward.

> For the Son of Man is going to come in his Father's glory with his angels, and then he will reward each person according to what he has done.
> **Matthew 16:27**

We will be evaluated for how faithful we have been. Not only will we be rewarded, we will also face judgment.

> Do not be deceived: God cannot be mocked. A man reaps what he sows. The one who sows to please his sinful nature, from that nature will reap destruction; the one who sows to please the Spirit, from the Spirit will reap eternal life.
> **Galatians 6:7-8**

If we want eternal life, we must be diligent in all our desires of Him. We must keep our thoughts faithfully focused on Him, and let our thoughts guide our actions. Remember, we are what we think.

> For we must all appear before the judgment seat of Christ, that each one may receive what is due him for the things done while in the body, whether good or bad.
> **II Corinthians 5:10**

Paul issues a call to us: our actions must reflect thoughts focused on Christ, because we will be held accountable in eternity. Paul is not saying that we are saved by our good works. We are saved solely by grace. But he reminds us that if we say we are followers of Christ, we must live as followers of Christ. Then we will appear before Christ at the time of judgment with joy in our hearts. This is the reason for our diligent focus on Him. Hear this promise:

> And without faith it is impossible to please God, because anyone who comes to him must believe that he exists and that he rewards those who earnestly seek him.
> **Hebrews 11:6**

Our faithfulness in keeping our mind focused on Christ will be rewarded in eternity. We must be faithful to Christ and never grow weary of imagining Him first.

May each of us choose to earnestly seek the mind of Christ, letting our thoughts of Him guide our actions and our life. May we be diligent in all our desires of Him. Now and for all eternity!

Changed Hearts, Changed Lives

IS IT ENOUGH TO KNOW ABOUT GOD? IS IT ENOUGH TO SEE CHRIST AS AN IMPORTANT HISTORICAL FIGURE? DOES OUR KNOWLEDGE OF GOD RELATE TO OUR LIFE?

The great theologian John Wesley struggled with these questions. In his early adult years, Wesley faithfully served as a priest in England and the United States. He committed himself to Bible study, prayer, fasting and serving others. He acknowledged that Jesus is the Son of God. But he studied only with his mind. He didn't understand in his heart that the promises of God were true for his every need.

Then, at age 35, he was transformed! During a meeting with fellow Christians in Aldersgate Street in London, Wesley had a deeply personal encounter with faith. While Martin Luther's preface to the commentary on the book of Romans was being read, Wesley became electrified.

Wesley called this experience a "quickening" in his soul. He said, "My heart was strangely warmed."

No longer were his beliefs merely intellectual. His mind was made new. In this Aldersgate experience, he realized the promises of God were true for him, and he developed a passionate relationship with the Lord.

Wesley went from being a dead theologian to a living Christian. He was turned upside down by realizing that what he knew in his head applied to his whole being. What he knew transformed how he lived!

It is a life-changing experience to be touched by God. It changed John Wesley. It has changed me. It can change you.

God welcomes each of us. He wants each of us to seek Him and to focus our heart and mind on Him. Then we can feel the presence of God awakening within us. He reaches us with His infinite love. He touches us with His wisdom, knowledge and discernment. Our heart is inclined to Him.

We are made new when we open our mind to the promises of God. He will touch us and transform us.

> I will give you a new heart and put a new spirit in you; I will remove from you your heart of stone and give you a heart of flesh. And I will put my Spirit in you and move you to follow my decrees and be careful to keep my laws.
> **Ezekiel 36:26-27**

What an awesome experience to have our heart touched by God! The active force of God's love is a critical agent of change. He heals us and freely bestows His love on us. He gives each of us a new heart, a heart that loves Him and loves to follow Him. Our imaginations are filled with Him.

Not only that, we now have His Spirit within us, guiding us, comforting us, supporting us and encouraging us. From the time we commit ourselves to God, we hear Him and know His presence through the Holy Spirit. Walking under the power of the Holy Spirit, we are obedient to His commands.

When God quickens us and transforms our faith, we are totally different. We have experienced *metanoia*. We don't try to improve or change our old ways of thinking and acting. The old ways are demolished! We are completely new!

> And we, who with unveiled faces all reflect the Lord's glory, are being transformed into his likeness with ever-increasing glory, which comes from the Lord, who is the Spirit.
> **II Corinthians 3:18**

When we embrace Christ as Lord and Savior, we put ourselves in God's hands. We let Him work through us to be transformed. We begin to reflect His glory. And as we are transformed, we go to greater and greater glory.

We have a new mind, a new hope, a new life! We are new beings in Christ. We are filled with His love, His perfection,

His perfect strength, His past grace, His present grace, His future grace.

> I pray that out of his glorious riches he may strengthen you with power through his Spirit in your inner being, so that Christ may dwell in your hearts through faith. And I pray that you, being rooted and established in love...may be filled to the measure of all the fullness of God.
> **Ephesians 3:16-17, 19**

Paul explains how Christ dwells in our heart by faith. God dips into His infinite riches and pours them into our heart, strengthening our inner thoughts with His Spirit. And that faith is rooted and grounded in His love for us.

These verses also explain our ultimate goal—to be filled with the fullness of God. Our goal of transformation, and our heartfelt longing, is to be filled with all the fullness of God.

Henry Brandt talks about the distinction between being transformed and being merely reformed. We try to reform ourselves by ourselves: physically by exercising, intellectually by pursuing higher learning in a college or university, spiritually by going to church. It's also an attitude we have toward others. For instance, I know a lot of people who have struggled with trying to "reform" their spouse.

We cannot be transformed as followers of Christ by ourselves. Our mind can never do it alone. It is only through the love and grace of God that we are transformed.

Transformation comes from the Spirit of God living within us, activating us. It ignites a spirit of peace that comes from total commitment—a spirit of *shalom*! *Shalom* is more than just a warm, fuzzy feeling. It is God working within us to create eternal peace and satisfaction in Him, through the guidance of the Holy Spirit.

Does that change who we are? Absolutely and completely!

> Those who look to him are radiant.
> **Psalm 34:5**

We will radiate Jesus Christ and what we've been given, now and for eternity—His grace, His love, His mercy, His joy, His forgiveness. We are finally made complete, not in ourselves, but through Christ.

There have been moments in my life when I've been participating in a worship service, for example, or enjoying God's world as I run, and a special awareness of Christ comes over me. It's a feeling I can't describe with words. But I am fully aware of God touching my heart in a deeply personal, transforming way.

When we are transformed, our imaginations of God are not just an intellectual exercise. We have a passion for Him. Not just intellectual knowledge, but an inner desire so that He affects all of our being.

We truly imagine God as our Creator, Redeemer and Sustainer. We see God as the one who gives us all blessings. We see that His love is the only love that can satisfy our heart. His forgiveness is the greatest acceptance we need. His wisdom is the greatest guide we have; we submit to His perfect will.

We see God's love overflowing into His grace, His grace into His mercy, His mercy into forgiveness for our sins—now and for eternity. This is the faith that transforms us!

The story of two of Jesus' disciples illustrates the difference between an intellectual faith and transforming faith.

In Jesus' last hours, two of His disciples sinned against Him. The first, Judas, went to the Jewish authorities and plotted the betrayal of Christ. Peter, after Jesus' arrest, was confronted about his relationship with Jesus and he denied knowing Christ.

Both despaired of their acts. But only one sought repentance.

Judas confessed his sin. "I have sinned," he said, "for I have betrayed innocent blood" (Matthew 27:4). But he didn't take the next step of faith. He couldn't seek God's mercy and forgiveness. Instead, he went away and hanged himself.

Peter, on the other hand, went back to the other disciples. In their company he discovered the empty tomb and the risen Lord. He rejoiced, but also knew he would be called to account for his actions.

After His resurrection, Jesus asked Peter three times, "Do you love me?" Three times, Peter said yes. And three times, Jesus gave Peter a critical role for the budding church: "Feed my sheep." Jesus, the good shepherd, entrusted the flock to a man who had denied knowing Him.

Peter had a transforming faith in Jesus Christ that was missing in Judas. Judas calculated his every move and intentionally rejected the Lord. Judas might have known, intellectually, that Jesus was Lord, but he lacked imagining a personal relationship with the living Lord.

Peter walked with Jesus differently. He had a transforming faith based on his personal relationship with Jesus.

Peter, in a moment of fear, rejected Jesus. But he later repented of his actions. His moment of doubt was erased by his life of faith.

He found his satisfaction in the person of Jesus Christ, and he could imagine the Lord's forgiving arms wrapped around him. He knew he had eternity stretching ahead of him with Jesus. And Jesus not only restored him, but gave him a place of great honor and responsibility.

A personal relationship built on transforming faith made the difference between Judas and Peter. It makes the difference in our life today. We can live, we can float, we can dwell, we can rest, we can be interwound with, we can be engulfed with the God of creation who made Himself known and visible in the person of Jesus Christ.

Satisfy us in the morning with your unfailing love,
that we may sing for joy and be glad all our days.
Psalm 90:14

This Psalm was written by Moses about the Israelites wandering in the wilderness. They had refused to believe God and go into the Promised Land. Moses prayed that the new generation would learn to find God as their true satisfaction.

How does this relate to us? On our own, we will never grasp this full measure of satisfaction. Our imaginations are too feeble. We will only be transformed when we are activated by faith, when we live full of faith that His promises are true for our life. Then we will have true satisfaction, contentment and joy!

Amazing Grace

IF GOD ASKED YOU WHY HE SHOULD LET YOU INTO HEAVEN, WHAT WOULD YOUR ANSWER BE? YOUR GOOD DEEDS OUT-WEIGH YOUR BAD? YOU'RE A MEMBER OF SUCH-AND-SUCH A CHURCH? YOU PRACTICE THE GOLDEN RULE? YOU TRY TO KEEP THE TEN COMMANDMENTS?

> For it is by grace you have been saved, through faith—and this not from yourselves, it is the gift of God—not by works, so that no one can boast.
> **Ephesians 2:8-9**

Jesus' encounter with a rich man in Matthew 19:16-20 explored these attitudes. This rich young ruler came to Jesus and asked Him, "What good thing must I do to get eternal life?" Jesus told him to keep the commandments: "Do not murder, do not commit adultery, do not steal, do not give false testimony, honor your father and mother, and love your neighbor as yourself."

The ruler said he'd done all that, but wondered what was still missing. He asked Jesus, "What do I still lack?" Jesus saw the man's thinking was in error. A person cannot earn eternal life by performing good works, by keeping the rules and the law. Jesus' response opened the man's eyes to his failure.

> Jesus answered, "If you want to be perfect, go, sell your possessions and give to the poor, and you will have treasure in heaven. Then come, follow me."
> **Matthew 19:21**

Jesus offers gracious hope to any who seek Him. All we must do is follow Him. Sadly, the man chose to not follow Christ.

When the young man heard this, he went away sad, because he had great wealth.
Matthew 19:22

The disciples, who had heard the whole conversation, were confused. They asked Jesus, "Who then can be saved?" Jesus reminded them of God's love and grace and power.

With man this is impossible, but with God all things are possible.
Matthew 19:26

Jesus makes it clear that salvation is never won by human attainment. Instead, salvation is available only by God's grace, when we accept Christ's atoning sacrifice. Faith is the gangplank to walking into God's grace.

Yet we keep trying to change God's rules. Our image of God is distorted. We can imagine that we have to work for our salvation—that we have to earn it through our deeds and our thoughts, rather than accepting His grace and trusting in His sovereignty. We can imagine that we have to give up all of life and become a stoic or ascetic. We can imagine that we have to live by many rules and be legalistic in our approach to others.

Remember, we can't show the Lord that we're worthy of salvation. All we'll show by our works is that we are imperfect people with faults, failings and false imaginations. We will never earn a position in eternity based on this faulty thinking.

None of us can meet the demands of God's law. None of us can earn His salvation by our obedience. We can fool ourselves and become perfectionists, as the Pharisees were. We can focus on what we should do, but still lack the love that makes His grace a reality in our life.

God did it all for us. Christ died on the cross so we would be freed from sin. He said, "It is finished," and we must receive His finished work to have forgiveness for our sins. That overwhelming act of love saves us. His generous sacrifice for our sins keeps us from despair that we'll never earn a place in heaven. We don't need to work for a slot. It is only the work of Christ on the cross that saves us. It's God's gift to us. And we don't need to despair that He can't redeem us. Nothing is too difficult for God.

If we imagine that we must prove ourselves to God (and in a similar way, that we have to prove ourselves to others), then surely we will be miserable, ill at ease and never find peace. Eventually, we will get tired of trying to prove ourselves, and we'll totally turn away from God. The imaginations of legalism lead to an empty heart that does not find satisfaction, fulfillment or redemption. Those imaginations ultimately lead to self-destruction.

We're not transformed by our own strength, but by faith in Him who is greater. We can envision faith activating God's grace and salvation. It is only by God's healing grace and forgiveness that we are made clean. We live in His grace. We find eternity in His grace. We find His presence in His grace.

> Remember that at that time you were separate from Christ, excluded from citizenship in Israel and foreigners to the covenants of the promise, without hope and without God in the world. But now in Christ Jesus you who once were far away have been brought near through the blood of Christ.
> **Ephesians 2:12-13**

The blood of Christ has the power to cleanse us of all the world's thoughts and actions. The blood of Christ has the power to transform us! Let us come to the Anointed One, the Messiah who mediates between God and man. We need to focus solely on Christ. When we see Him as the essential element of our being, our thoughts and actions will follow.

It is only through God's grace that He loves us enough to touch us and restore us—as wretched and sinful as we all are.

We all have failings. We all have sins. God's grace cleanses us. His grace washes away our past, which is filled with failures and mistakes. God's grace upholds us today, as we struggle to take on imaginations focused on Him and leave worldly thoughts behind. His grace will provide for us tomorrow and for eternity. We have His grace forever!

When God restores our heart through His grace, we're deeply and intimately bound to Him. We begin the journey toward a life that is more abundant, peaceful and joyful. We focus our mind and heart on the One who saves us, redeems us and transforms us. Praise be to God for His matchless grace! Amen!

A New Perspective

WHAT DO YOU THINK HAPPENS TO US WHEN WE DIE? DO YOU THINK ABOUT DEATH'S APPROACH? DO YOU KEEP BUSY IN YOUR DAILY LIFE WITH WORK AND FAMILY AND ACTIVITIES TO KEEP FROM THINKING ABOUT DEATH? DO YOU BELIEVE HEAVEN IS REAL, BUT IRRELEVANT?

I know a lot of people don't like to think about death and what will happen to them. But all of us have an appointment with death. There is no place we can hide.

The Bible tells me that I will spend eternity with God through my relationship with Jesus Christ. Death to this life is just the graduation to heaven.

In fact, I'm already living, just a bit, of that eternal life here on earth. And because He loves me that much, He will take care of me every day. This is the power that transforms my imaginations!

The Apostle Paul had that kind of transforming faith. It allowed him to write these words while in prison, not knowing whether he would be executed or allowed to live.

For to me, to live is Christ and to die is gain.
Philippians 1:21

Paul knew that heaven is real. More than that, to him it had deep relevance. Heaven is more than anything this world has to offer. More than life itself!

Heaven is eternity in the presence of the living God. Paul could live in anticipation of his time on earth and his time in heaven.

How do you imagine eternity? Here's one image I like to use. Our Father owns the land on both sides of the river. The side we're on now is the life we live in this world. The other side of the river is eternity. In this image, I can see myself eternally cared for by Him. My image of eternity is positive, not negative. It allows me to be strong and courageous when facing death. It has comforted me when fellow believers have died.

God has promised to keep us in His presence. We can look at death without fear. That imagination is what allowed Paul to write these words:

> Where, O death, is your victory?
> Where, O death, is your sting?
> …But thanks be to God! He gives us the victory through our Lord Jesus Christ.
> **I Corinthians 15:55, 57**

The prison doors that locked us in worldly thinking are shattered! Christ's resurrection frees us from our sins and frees us from death. We have the eternal bliss of being engulfed with Him. What an imagination of the heart!

John Bunyan described this so beautifully in his book *The Pilgrim's Progress*. Bunyan told the story of Christian, the pilgrim whose only goal was the Celestial City—eternity with God.

Christian encountered trials and temptations along the way and found loyal companions who encouraged him. Finally, he saw the city, glorious to behold. But before he could enter the gate, he had to cross a turbulent river and there was no bridge.

The River Jordan is the River of Death. It is a treacherous crossing.

Christian entered the river and the waves crashed over his head. He was turned upside down. He cried out, afraid he would die and never reach the city. And he found strength in his faith that God would provide.

He recalled the promise God made to the people of Israel through Isaiah:

When you pass through the waters,
    I will be with you;
and when you pass through the rivers,
    they will not sweep over you.
Isaiah 43:2

Once his faith was firmly established, the river became shallow, and Christian easily finished his crossing. His faith led to peace. And that peace directed him toward God, wanting to touch the Lord in the Celestial City. He went through the gate and entered the paradise of God.

Through Jesus, death is swallowed up forever! Death is conquered eternally. Death is no longer a barrier between us and God, but is a doorway to Him. When we step into heaven, we'll say, "This is my God! I've waited for Him. I rejoice in Him."

As the prophet Isaiah wrote:

In that day they will say,
"Surely this is our God;
    we trusted in him, and he saved us.
This is the Lord, we trusted in him;
    let us rejoice and be glad in his salvation."
Isaiah 25:9

We know Him now, and we look forward to that day of seeing Him face-to-face in heaven. Everything else is trivial. We will be with Him for eternity! We have eternal victory through Christ!

I have a friend whose body is dying. Yet he is full of peace and knows he will be engulfed with God for eternity. The light of the Celestial City, of heaven, allows him to imagine eternity. That vision keeps him going, even through cancer treatments and as he faces death.

Eternity is where we put all our hopes, our goals, our cares and our concerns. Where there's Christ, there's hope. Where there's Christ, there's joy.

I've seen this joy in fellow believers who were dying. They weren't afraid. They weren't worried. They were actually ecstatic toward the time of their death. They knew, they had seen, Christ's hands carrying them toward an eternity of perfect peace and joy!

> If we live, we live to the Lord; and if we die, we die to the Lord. So, whether we live or die, we belong to the Lord.
> **Romans 14:8**

What a promise! We belong to the Lord! We have eternity with Him!

For me, believing this means life is more exciting. Getting up in the morning and going to bed at night, eating my daily meals and going through my daily activities is a richer experience.

This eternal perspective becomes the focus for our life, the foundation for our life. We no longer see ourselves in the same way.

We now live in anticipation of His eternal presence. We make all of our decisions based on that premise. We see that our life on earth is short and soon passes away. But we're with the eternal God forever!

Can we follow the example of John Wesley? When he was quickened by the Holy Spirit, he had a new way of looking at the world. He saw eternity with Christ—an eternal relationship, an eternal feast with his Lord and Savior.

> On this mountain the Lord Almighty will prepare
> a feast of rich food for all peoples,
> a banquet of aged wine—
> the best of meats and the finest of wines.
> On this mountain he will destroy
> the shroud that enfolds all peoples,
> the sheet that covers all nations;
> he will swallow up death forever.
> The Sovereign Lord will wipe away the tears from all faces;
> he will remove the disgrace of his people from all the earth.
> The Lord has spoken.
> **Isaiah 25:6-8**

These verses are rich with the themes that help us imagine the Lord. Isaiah is telling us about the presence of Jesus on earth and His death and resurrection. Through Him, we have seats at the table of the richest, most exquisite feast—a feast greater than physical food and drink. It's a feast in which God is our portion. And we are at this feast for eternity.

This contradicts the consumer culture in which we live. We're barraged by media messages telling us to live for today, to get as much as we can, as quickly as we can. We're told to measure our success by dollar signs and to compare ourselves with those around us.

> But you, man of God, flee from all this, and pursue right-eousness, godliness, faith, love, endurance and gentleness. Fight the good fight of the faith. Take hold of the eternal life to which you were called when you made your good confession in the presence of many witnesses.
> **I Timothy 6:11-12**

When we focus on eternal imaginations, we can understand better how little the possessions and measures of worldly success matter.

We can point ourselves toward eternity with Him. We can work enough to be satisfied in our daily lives and not be consumed by the cares of the present day.

Instead, we are consumed by our focus on our future with Him—a future that begins now as we are engulfed in His presence.

> But one thing I do: Forgetting what is behind and straining toward what is ahead, I press on toward the goal to win the prize for which God has called me heavenward in Christ Jesus.
> **Philippians 3:13-14**

The prize for which we run is not ours; it is Christ's prize. The Lord wants our mind in union with His so we can live in eternity with Him, fully engulfed in His presence. The true prize is our eternal relationship with God through the person of Jesus Christ.

The hustle and bustle of everyday life sometimes makes it easy to forget eternity, but eternity must be the backdrop for every part of our temporary life on this planet.

George Gilder said, "Men lust, but they do not know what for. They wander, and lose track of the goal. They fight and compete, but they forget the prize. They spread seed, but spurn the seasons of growth. They chase power and glory, but miss the meaning of life."

Hear the words of Jesus:

Do not store up for yourselves treasures on earth, where moth and rust destroy, and where thieves break in and steal. But store up for yourselves treasures in heaven, where moth and rust do not destroy, and where thieves do not break in and steal. For where your treasure is, there your heart will be also.
Matthew 6:19-21

Remember that rich young ruler, who couldn't give up his worldly possessions to follow Christ? The love for the material goods of this world kept him from following Christ.

Is it the same with us? Do we trust God to provide treasures in heaven? Can we give up the material goods of this world? Jesus asks all of us to prefer heavenly treasures to all the wealth and riches this world offers. When we open our arms to embrace Christ, the possessions of this world fall away. We can't cling to them if we are reaching out to Christ, now and for eternity.

Because we have that eternal imagination in our mind, we have a new outlook in our daily life—we have a new satisfaction and contentment. We have genuine peace.

I've seen people in situations that would seem unbearable. Yet their satisfaction in the Lord, through their transforming faith in His eternal provision, supports them and guides them. Their imaginations are centered on the Lord and on His desire that we find our greatest delight in Him. Their actions reflect the spiritual wisdom that flows from faith in God's promises. They have a genuine sense of satisfaction, and they are filled with hope, peace and joy. They have grasped the eternal vision of God for their purpose in life.

When we're filled with God's eternal perspective, we concentrate on the inner workings of our heart, our mindset and imaginations and attitudes. We see more clearly how we fit into God's eternal plans. We live looking forward to eternal fellowship with God. Author John Piper refers to God's "future grace"—where we're engulfed with His presence forever and alive with Him forever.

God says to each of us, "Come up here and be with Me; come up here and be My child; come up here and be like the Savior, and be in My presence forever."

May each of us join God in the eternal feast of His blessings—now and forever!

The Motivation Equation

LET'S IMAGINE OURSELVES AS HAVING RECEIVED NOW AND FOR ETERNITY EVERY BLESSING GOD HAS FOR US—HIS LOVE, HIS MERCY, HIS GRACE, HIS FORGIVENESS, HIS JOY. DO WE LET THOSE THINGS MOTIVATE OUR LIFE DAY BY DAY? OR DOES SOMETHING ELSE MOTIVATE US? MORE MONEY, MORE POWER, MORE COMFORTS, MORE RECOGNITION, MORE LEISURE TIME OR MORE SEXUAL RELATIONSHIPS?

> The acts of the sinful nature are obvious: sexual immorality, impurity and debauchery; idolatry and witchcraft; hatred, discord, jealousy, fits of rage, selfish ambition, dissensions, factions and envy; drunkenness, orgies, and the like.
> **Galatians 5:19-21**

Paul describes four categories of worldly, or vain, imaginations in those verses: the sensual, the sorcery, the substance and the social.

The sensual can be extremely normal. But when the sensual strays from a godly focus, it becomes abnormal. It can destroy us.

Sorcery includes worship of all kinds of things that are not of God. Any worship is abnormal and sinful when it isn't focused on the true God.

Substance, and substance abuse, are very common. Substances can be food, drink, tobacco or any substance that takes over our spirit and takes us away from God.

The fourth category, social, is the strife that takes over when we lose our love for God and for others.

These four stem from a fifth "s": selfishness. Do we have an eternal perspective or are we filled with worldly thoughts? Worldly thoughts stem from selfish motives—a focus on our own desires, rather than focusing on God's eternal grace and provision. We think we can rely solely on ourselves. No longer do we find our satisfaction in God's promises. Instead, we isolate ourselves from Him and we plant the seed for additional trials and temptations.

My good friend Dr. William Standish Reed, president of Christian Medical Foundation International, says there are two systems that shape us: clinging to the dust and clinging to God. When we cling to the dust we're holding on to earthly appetites. We have the values of this world—the desire for material goods, material symbols of worldly success. When we're clinging to God, we have a new heavenly appetite, the Word of God and the eternal Kingdom of Heaven.

"Healing, blessing and wholeness, creativity, godly love, joy unspeakable, and a magnificent inward spiritual rejoicing are the products of the spiritual life rather than of the natural life," Dr. Reed says.

If we want the transforming power of Christ in our life, we must reject the self-centered thinking that the world promotes. We must keep an eternal perspective. That means we must be willing to totally change our way of thinking. We must be willing to do away with our worldly thoughts and surrender to Him.

We are filled with lasting imaginations of peace, joy, thanksgiving, hope and love when we focus on Jesus Christ. We don't just think about Him in passing, as we go about our daily routines. When we are transformed by faith, we must let His thoughts be our thoughts, His mindset be our mindset, His imaginations be our imaginations. We surrender our selfishness to seek Him.

> Your attitude should be the same as that of Christ Jesus:
> Who, being in very nature God,
> did not consider equality with God something
>   to be grasped,

but made himself nothing,
taking the very nature of a servant,
being made in human likeness.
And being found in appearance as a man,
he humbled himself
and became obedient to death—
even death on a cross!
Therefore God exalted him to the highest place
and gave him the name that is above every name,
that at the name of Jesus every knee should bow,
in heaven and on earth and under the earth,
and every tongue confess that Jesus Christ is Lord,
to the glory of God the Father.
Philippians 2:5-11

Our mind is changed, our imaginations are changed, so that we imagine Jesus, we think Jesus and we live Jesus. We change the filter of our minds. We no longer look through a filter of worldly desires and selfishness. We see through the filter of Christ's mind.

Submit yourselves, then, to God. Resist the devil, and he will flee from you.
James 4:7

Christianity is the opposite of selfishness. We must be completely unselfish to hand over our life to Him. We must surrender our heart, our mind, our will, our sense of independence and pride to Him. "Self" must be on the cross. Imagine our earthly thoughts, our worldly imaginations, dying with Christ on that cross. We must die to self and live in Him.

If anyone would come after me, he must deny himself and take up his cross and follow me. For whoever wants to save his life will lose it, but whoever loses his life for me will find it.
Matthew 16:24-25

Death to self is essential if we are to surrender to Him. Death to self destroys the false imaginations that tell us our own frail, feeble human powers are sufficient to provide for us. We refuse to accept the vain imaginations, restless thoughts and worries of this world. We abandon ourselves to Christ. We walk in joy and love as the children of God.

When our imaginations are focused on Christ, we see the world in a different way. Our motivation is no longer to achieve earthly status and success. Our motivation is the gorgeous beauty of being with the Lord for eternity. We see eternity reaching out before us.

Surrender to Him means we're putting our roots down in the love and mercy of the Lord. We must live with the images of surrender to God and then act on those images. We no longer have a sinful mind, but we have the mind of Christ. We must think and act like God to truly be His children.

Surrender makes us more reflective so that we seek His will and unite our mind with His. We don't give up our thought processes. We aren't mindless children who follow with blind obedience. We take the simple truth of His grace and think it through so that science, knowledge of God and God Himself all merge together in a meaningful relationship. With a simple, yet strong, faith we have a reflective, informed understanding of the mind of God as it is revealed to us in the Bible.

The more we let Him nurture us and guide us, the greater our transformation will be. We receive His love, His grace, His forgiveness and His strength. We align our mind and our thoughts with Him. The fruit we produce—our actions— stems from the thoughts focused on Him. We must apply His mind in our daily life and let our actions and works come out of our state of praise and worship to God.

What we own in life isn't important. What owns us is very important. Does our desire for worldly success own us? Or have we truly surrendered ourselves to Him?

Taking on the mindset of Jesus, surrendering to His will, transforms us. When we take on Jesus in our person, we have to see life differently. We see it through the heart and mind of Jesus. We don't merely include Him as part of our thinking. We let His will permeate our being.

Do not conform any longer to the pattern of this world,
but be transformed by the renewing of your mind. Then
you will be able to test and approve what God's will is—his
good, pleasing and perfect will.
Romans 12:2

Christ can renew our mind. His transforming power helps us replace negative, worldly thoughts and imaginations with His eternal wisdom. We are able to look to Jesus and focus on His love, His peace, His thanksgiving and His forgiveness. Again, the word for this renewal is *metanoia*, a changed mind, a transformed mind.

We give up the mind of the world to have the mind of Christ. We're at peace because we're satisfied with Jesus. We no longer need the world. We walk in the power of the Holy Spirit rather than trying to live directing our own way.

Yet selfishness remains the root of so many of our struggles and problems. Look at one encounter between the prophet Jeremiah and the people of Israel caused by selfishness.

My people have committed two sins:
They have forsaken me,
the spring of living water,
and have dug their own cisterns,
broken cisterns that cannot hold water.
Jeremiah 2:13

Jeremiah reproaches the people of Israel for turning away from God. First, they turned from worshipping God to worshipping idols. They turned from the living God, the "fountain of life" (Psalm 36:9). They have tried to create their own water.

Symbolically, they were seeking a source of life that excluded God. In a practical sense, they built their own cisterns for water. But those cisterns didn't work. When the people went to them for water, all they found was mud and muck. When they went to the idols for spiritual water, they came away empty because the idols were false gods.

The people's selfishness ended up hurting them. The cisterns raised false hopes about drinkable water. The idols offered empty promises.

Their selfishness was the opposite of faith. They no longer trusted God to provide and thought they needed to take care of themselves. As a result, they found themselves isolated from God.

At what times are we selfish? We don't always need cisterns to provide drinking water, but do we envision ourselves relying on the "spring of living water" to sustain us? How often do we turn from a mindset of trusting in God to imaginations of selfishness?

One of Frank Sinatra's most famous songs is *My Way*. The song's lyrics talk about a person making his own choices, not following someone else's rules. One of Sinatra's nicknames was the Chairman of the Board. In his life he certainly made up his own rules as he went along, for better or worse. And he developed quite a reputation.

Now think about this in relationship to God. God needs to be the Chairman of the Board in our life. We have to desire to live His way, not our own way. When we fall away from following God's directions and from godly ideas, we are arrogant. Then we follow our own desires and engage in actions that are not of the Lord. Our arrogance can lead to self-destruction. So arrogance is one of the most ungodly characteristics, and we must overcome it.

> There are six things the Lord hates,
> seven that are detestable to him:
> haughty eyes,
> a lying tongue,
> hands that shed innocent blood,
> a heart that devises wicked schemes,
> feet that are quick to rush into evil,
> a false witness who pours out lies
> and a man who stirs up dissension among brothers.
> **Proverbs 6:16-19**

This is a very vivid description of what God hates most. Our desire for control, our arrogance that we can live without the Word of God, leads our heart and our imaginations away from Him. We've lost our firm footing of faith in God's promises. In our arrogance, we rebel against the Word of God.

We cannot find genuine satisfaction until we reject our desire to control our life and remember His promises to provide for us. We need to remember His eternal promises.

> "For I know the plans I have for you," declares the Lord, "plans to prosper you and not to harm you, plans to give you hope and a future."
> **Jeremiah 29:11**

There's an Old Testament story about a king who wanted to be in control. King Nebuchadnezzar was a brilliant military tactician and skilled in international diplomacy. During his reign, the Chaldean empire flourished. He even rebuilt the city of Babylon. With its paved roads, canals and temples, the city was magnificent.

Nebuchadnezzar occupied Judah, including Jerusalem, deporting King Jehoiakim to Babylon. He also took hostages back to Babylon, including Daniel.

Then one day, as King Nebuchadnezzar was walking on the roof of his palace, his pride got the better of him and he said,

> "Is not this the great Babylon I have built as the royal residence, by my mighty power and for the glory of my majesty?" The words were still on his lips when a voice came from heaven, "This is what is decreed for you, King Nebuchadnezzar: Your royal authority has been taken from you. You will be driven away from people and will live with the wild animals; you will eat grass like cattle. Seven times will pass by for you until you acknowledge that the Most High is sovereign over the kingdoms of men and gives them to anyone he wishes."
> **Daniel 4:30-32**

The king wanted to get the credit for all the good things of the kingdom. God's punishment of the earthly king's imaginations of pride and control was swift. Nebuchadnezzar lost his honor as a king and as a man. He lost his kingdom, his subjects and his reason. He became like an animal, running wild on all fours into the fields and woods. The one who thought he was greater than the average person was made to be less, eating grass like animals.

Nebuchadnezzar was insecure and selfish. We lose, too, because of our pride when we have imaginations of being in control.

It's easy for us to start taking the credit for all the blessings we have and all our accomplishments and activities and awards. As a doctor, it's easy to say, "Oh, look what I've accomplished! Look how many people I've helped. Look at this great practice I've built."

It's easy for people in any profession, and it's human nature, to want to take pride in our accomplishments. But it's also far too easy to lose sight of God's sovereignty and His power in helping us achieve success in our life. We may think we've done great things by our own power and think of ourselves as powerful. Our pride and arrogance bring us down.

There's good news in the story of Nebuchadnezzar. God didn't leave the king running wild in the fields. Nebuchadnezzar recovered his senses; his sanity was restored. No longer did he look down to the earth to provide, as an animal does. He lifted his eyes up as a man, as a humble petitioner for God's mercy, and saw the glory and majesty of the eternal God who rules over us all. He praised God, saying:

[God's] dominion is an eternal dominion;
his kingdom endures from generation to generation.
All the peoples of the earth are regarded as nothing.
He does as he pleases with the powers of heaven
and the peoples of the earth.
No one can hold back his hand or say to him:
"What have you done?"
Daniel 4:34-35

Nebuchadnezzar humbled himself and glorified God. Then he was restored as king, with added wisdom. He more fully understood that only God is in control, and Nebuchadnezzar praised and honored the king of heaven.

We need to do the same. We can find our complete satisfaction in God's promises. He has all the power. We can do all things through Him. We find ourselves in Him.

We won't be perfect. We will struggle to surrender ourselves every day. We will be tempted by vain imaginations.

As Nebuchadnezzar did, it's so important that we are able to admit when we've done wrong. I recently broke a leg skiing. I just had to admit, I was going too fast and had my bindings too tight. I paid for wanting the thrill of going fast and being with my buddies.

We have to admit our wrong desires. We must say, "Lord, I'm way off track in the way my mind's aligned. Align me to Jesus."

We also need to let go of the past—our successes and shortcomings, our fears about failure, the consequences of sin in our life, our unmet needs, our unresolved feelings and memories, our rejections. Dwelling on past history distorts our patterns of thinking and doesn't allow His perfect vision complete access to our thoughts.

We must fix our imaginations on an attitude of surrender. We must dedicate our mind to surrendering to God.

> Is not my house right with God?
> Has he not made with me an everlasting covenant,
> arranged and secured in every part?
> Will he not bring to fruition my salvation
> and grant me my every desire?
> But evil men are all to be cast aside like thorns,
> which are not gathered with the hand.
> **II Samuel 23:5-6**

In these verses, King David was disappointed that his family did not love and serve God as much as they should. David anticipated there would be trouble in his family after his death. But God's love had changed David. David knew it could change others, if they surrendered to Him. How much more difficult it would be for his family if they continued to rebel against the one and only God.

It's still that way today. We can never realize God's transforming love if we are in a state of rebellion.

Yet David also knew that he had a covenant with God. And like those of us who receive God's *agape* love and pass it on, who receive His forgiveness and pass it on, who receive Jesus and pass Him on—we have a covenant.

Now, there are people who go to church, who love the church, who do all kinds of good deeds for the church and in the name of the church. They go to the Lord and say they are sorry for their sin. But then they go back and commit the same sin without a changed mind. And again, they have to go back to the Lord and say they are sorry.

Saying we're sorry isn't enough. We have to live out repentance, a changed heart, a changed life, to truly feel the power of God in us. It's OK to feel remorse when we've sinned, when we've made a mistake. But remorse isn't enough.

We need to repent. Then we need to return our mind to Him and let Christ-like thoughts direct our actions. We are what we think. We have not fully repented unless our actions reflect a God-centered mind.

Paul described this when he spoke before King Agrippa.

> So then, King Agrippa, I was not disobedient to the vision from heaven. First to those in Damascus, then to those in Jerusalem and in all Judea, and to the Gentiles also, I preached that they should repent and turn to God and prove their repentance by their deeds.
> **Acts 26:19-20**

Remember. Repent. Return. This process of life is the essence of Christianity. We will stray from our sense of satisfaction in Him. We will try to create our own satisfaction in worldly terms. We will try to do it our own way. But our true satisfaction is found only in an eternal relationship with the person of Jesus Christ.

Remember the height from which you have fallen!
Repent and do the things you did at first.
Revelation 2:5

We remember our true foundation—transforming faith in the promises of God. We repent of our sins. And then we return to living a life that glorifies God, in our thoughts as well as in our actions.

Repentance is turning toward Christ, not just turning away from the world. We haven't met eternal life until we meet God and trust Him and submit ourselves to Him. Life is repentance to God and living in His presence.

What a dynamic imagination! Turning ourselves, focusing ourselves fully on the redeeming power of Christ's blood and His ultimate sacrifice for each of us. Hear His promise:

The Lord is not slow in keeping his promise, as some understand slowness. He is patient with you, not wanting anyone to perish, but everyone to come to repentance.
II Peter 3:9

God wants each of us to repent and turn to Him! He offers salvation to all. He knows we will perish without Him.

Life truly begins when we surrender to Christ at Calvary, when we marvel at God's matchless grace. Only then do we find true satisfaction. Only then do we realize the power of the resurrection is ours for eternity!

The good news is that we can pursue the mind of God every day! We can claim our eternal life in Him every day! We can renew our relationship with Him every day! We must live before the Lord Jesus, our King, and let Him be our joy and portion, our King and Master.

May each of us let go of our selfishness and cling to Christ, surrendering our life to Him with reckless abandon. We remember, repent and return. Our new, surrendered self lives with Him. We live in the power of the resurrection, the love of the Trinity and His presence for eternity!

Resting in God

THE KEY PRINCIPLE TO STAYING FOCUSED ON GOD IS TO BE FAITHFUL, AND KEEP HIS ETERNAL PERSPECTIVE BEFORE US EVERY DAY. THIS IS IMPOSSIBLE TO DO IF WE THINK WE MUST RELY SOLELY ON OUR OWN POWER TO STAY DISCIPLINED. SO IMAGINE THIS ATTITUDE ANOTHER WAY: IMAGINE TAKING ON THE MIND OF CHRIST. THEN WE CAN SEE HOW HE WORKS TO TRANSFORM US. WE CAN SEE HOW THE HOLY SPIRIT INFUSES US AND ENGULFS OUR HEART AND OUR MIND.

When we take on the mind of Christ, much of the struggle is taken away in life and we are able to truly rest in Him. We still face difficulties, trials and temptations. But we can trust in Him, lean on Him, rely on Him, depend on Him and rest in Him at all times. We have the true images of Him as Jehovah-Jireh, as our Father, as our Shepherd, as the One who provides.

One of the most important attitudes of the mind is to totally surrender to God, yet totally concentrate on Him. It sounds like a paradox. Let me give you an example.

In golf, a player must fully concentrate on the game, yet be totally relaxed so the body performs well. If your wrist is too tight when you swing the club, your wrist won't move correctly. When you hit the ball it doesn't go very far—or sometimes it doesn't even go in the right direction.

In the operating room, we have to concentrate on the procedure. But if we're worried and nervous and uptight, the operation will seem more difficult to perform.

In skiing the term for this mindset is anticipation. You have to concentrate to go safely down the hill, but you also have to trust your skills and gravity to bring you through the turns safely to the bottom. You anticipate the turn, plant your pole, pull your body and surrender to the forces of gravity and your own reflexes, which bring you through the turn.

When I'm skiing, I'll go down the slopes with my wife, praying, "Lord, let us surrender, surrender, surrender." We surrender as we go down the hill.

The only way to truly relax through life's turns is to be surrendered to God. It is His will that guides our life. We live through Him and for Him. We align ourselves with Him. Let's see how Paul's attitude exemplifies this:

I have been crucified with Christ and I no longer live, but Christ lives in me. The life I live in the body, I live by faith in the Son of God, who loved me and gave himself for me.
Galatians 2:20

No longer do we act solely through our own efforts. We let the Lord's strength and vision guide us. We keep our eyes on the goal: getting down the hill or living the life of Christ. In anticipation in Christ, we have to look into His eyes, drop our body down and let God-given strength empower us. We need to let the power of God's gravity pull us through as we plant our pole. Then we get the automatic spring as we come through and turn into the fall line. The next turn spontaneously takes place with no effort.

In skiing, there is no effort at all when the proper technique is used: anticipating, planting the pole, letting gravity pull you into the hill and around the turn, and relaxing through all the motion. If you don't relax, your muscles get tense and don't stay flexible. Then you fall.

As Christians, we can't get tense. We must stay relaxed. Our satisfaction in God's promise to provide gives us this attitude, imagination and mindset.

When we've surrendered completely with our "pole plant," we rise up with total faith that He will continually provide for us. When we rest in the Lord and totally relinquish ourselves, we are at peace with our God, ourselves, our work and others. It requires being able to trust, being thankful and believing. We then are amazed at the strength God gives us. We are truly enabled to live by faith and die to self. Look again at Galatians 2:20:

> I have been crucified with Christ and I no longer live, but Christ lives in me. The life I live in the body, I live by faith in the Son of God, who loved me and gave himself for me.

Plant our pole: "I have been crucified with Christ." We give in to His gravity, His power, His pressure: "Christ lives in me." He is the point of reference for our body, our mind, our muscles, our decisions. Our thoughts are His thoughts. His will is our will. As we put down the pole, we rise up and live in this flesh by faith. We make the turn, completing Galatians 2:20: "Faith in Him who loved me and gave Himself for me."

When we work together in a joyous rhythm of enjoyment in life in Christ, even our body can be at peace, totally relaxed doing everything through God's power.

Unfortunately we don't always live according to Galatians 2:20. I know a man whose life was the opposite of this rest in Christ. He was the manager of a very important corporation. He believed and practiced Christian ethics in business and was completely trustworthy. Yet he didn't know how to relax. He wasn't able to enjoy life. He was the perfect example of a good body being destroyed by a brain that wasn't allowing the body to do as it should.

In life we simply rise up with God's strength, knowing and believing the Lord will complete everything He has started, including the turns in our life.

A beautiful image of the Lord illustrates how we should rest in Him.

> I am the true vine, and my Father is the gardener. He cuts off every branch in me that bears no fruit, while every branch that does bear fruit he prunes so that it will be even more fruitful. You are already clean because of the

word I have spoken to you. Remain in me, and I will remain in you. No branch can bear fruit by itself; it must remain in the vine. Neither can you bear fruit unless you remain in me. **John 15:1-4**

We need in our mind the imagination of Jesus as the vine, nourishing us, feeding us, directing our growth. Our life as a branch is one of rest. We can't push the vine, telling it where we want to go or what we want to do. We can't provide for ourselves. If we're cut off from the vine, we'll perish. When we don't abide in Him, we become very barren and we burn out. All we can do is joyfully rest in union with the vine of life.

Trust in the Lord with all your heart
and lean not on your own understanding;
in all your ways acknowledge him,
and he will make your paths straight.
Proverbs 3:5

Every day, all we can do is say, "Lord, I want to depend on you in everything I do." We need to think of ourselves as a lamb, dependent for our life on our shepherd, the living God.

When we rest in our relationship with the living, transforming Lord we aren't slothful and lazy. Resting in Him produces real fruit: true peace and His spirit of love and service. We desire to be closer to Him, but we are resting in the Spirit. We will face periods of pruning, times of trouble and hardship. But our attachment to the vine, our relationship with Jesus Christ, will continue to nourish and sustain us.

When we trust in the Lord and rest in Him, we glorify Him. He gets glory and we get joy!

Communion with Christ

IS SAYING WE'RE SURRENDERING OUR WILL TO GOD ENOUGH? HOW DO WE KNOW WHETHER WE'RE RESTING IN HIM? DOES HAVING AN ETERNAL VIEW OF OUR LIFE FREE US FROM DAILY RESPONSIBILITY?

These questions boil down to a more basic issue: Do we think of God as a remote, distant being or is He our partner in daily living?

None of these other factors are true and meaningful unless Jesus is alive in our life every day. Our responsibility is to daily continue in faith, for without faith there is no relationship with the living God.

Blessed are those who have learned to acclaim you,
who walk in the light of your presence, O Lord.
Psalm 89:15

This verse speaks of a spiritual walk with God. It tells us we are blessed when we learn to have that daily relationship. In fact, there are many verses in the Bible that talk about walking with God, about believing in Jesus' presence in our life every day. We find our full measure of satisfaction when we walk daily in that Spirit.

Several authors have described this walk. C.S. Lewis would say we are in meaningful acceleration when we are in harmony with the character of God. John Piper would say we are glorifying God by enjoying Him forever. Hudson Taylor would say we have a balance between being totally at peace with God and desiring to be closer to Him. Jonathan Edwards would say our mind is aligned with God.

All those definitions describe a eucharistic lifestyle. In certain churches, the Eucharist is the Lord's Supper, or Communion. The eucharistic lifestyle is an imagination of the mind in which we are in constant communion with the Lord, constantly in prayer with the Lord, constantly worshipping and praising the Lord.

The Old Testament tells us about Enoch. When Enoch was 65 years old, he became the father of Methuselah. He lived another 300 years and had other children. Genesis tells us that Enoch "walked with God; then he was no more, because God took him away" (Genesis 5:24).

On his down days, Enoch sought God's help for encouragement in his disappointments with life. On his up days, he praised God for His great goodness. Day in and day out, year in and year out, for more than 300 years he walked with God. God was the essence of his life. Enoch had a personal relationship with God. They were in constant fellowship. Then Enoch was translated into the presence of God because he walked in His steps and grew intimate with Him.

Do we have a habit of walking with Him? Or just talking at Him? When we are intimate with Him, we fellowship with the Lord Jesus. We renew our mind, especially through daily prayer and the study of His Word, which transforms us to His image in all areas of our life.

Bible knowledge is important, but more important is satisfaction with the person of Jesus Christ in our life. Praise is important, but more important is satisfaction with the person of Jesus Christ in our life. Prayer is important, but more important is satisfaction with the person of Jesus Christ in our life.

Satisfaction comes through a relationship, through daily communion with God. He wants an intimate relationship of love with us. And Christ is the key. Through Christ we have a relationship with our Creator. We know God through Christ, and through Christ we are known to God. We must be as a child seeking His heart. Our relationship with God is one of surrender and a desire to have intimate fellowship with Him. We are engulfed and interwound with His presence. Then we enter into the fullness of God!

I know God as the one who saves the worst of sinners. Every day I strive to keep Him intimately involved in every aspect of my life. He totally interwinds the past, the present and the future. He holds all the forces of the universe in the palm of His hand. He demonstrated that power by being nailed on the cross, carrying all the sins of the world. The only sinless soul died for all of my sins and all of your sins.

It's important that we don't think of God as some small, remote concept who created the world, sent Jesus to save it, and then observes us from a distance.

God is within us and around us. He gives us a future to believe in. He allows us to do all things through that same Christ who suffered and died on the cross, and now lives to redeem and strengthen us.

Think about the first time you fell in love. Remember that initial glow, that feeling of walking on air because you loved someone? Maybe they loved you in return, maybe not. But your life was changed because you were in love. The air you breathed was different, food tasted different, your sleep patterns changed, everything about you and around you seemed different because you were in love.

Now, think about how the relationship changed with the person you loved. As the two of you developed a relationship, what happened? Did the love grow stronger? Did the passion burn brighter? Did you grow more committed to that person? Or, as you grew to know them better, did you become less interested, until the relationship withered away?

Let's apply all this to our relationship with God. I've seen many people who fall head over heels in love with God when He first touches their heart. Their face shines; they have a different kind of glow. Others are transformed quietly, subtly, but they love Him deeply.

> Those who look to him are radiant;
> their faces are never covered with shame.
> **Psalm 34:5**

When God first touches us, and we surrender to Him, we take the first step on the path to an eternal relationship of love. Christ saves us. Our mindset from that point determines our relationship with Him.

I recently heard the Rev. Larry Jackson of Clinton, N.C., give a sermon about our relationship with Christ. He asked the question: Are we married to Jesus or are we just trying to "shack up" with Him?

Think about the implications. Are we passionate about Christ or are we half-hearted about our love for Him? Are we committed to Christ or do we just enjoy the relationship until we find some other interest? Are we trying to get something for nothing out of this relationship or are we interested in surrendering ourselves to it? Have we changed where we live? Have we changed our name? Do we want to know more about Christ or are we reluctant to devote time to build the relationship?

Godly imaginations of the mind can only be developed in a deeply personal relationship with God. It's almost like getting married and then learning what married life is all about. Our satisfaction in Christ, our imaginations of Him, are developing daily. But underneath is the desire for a relationship with Him more than anything else. The daily development may be fast or slow, but we develop because we are faithfully and fervently focused on Him.

> You will keep in perfect peace
> him whose mind is steadfast,
> because he trusts in you.
> **Isaiah 26:3**

A steadfast mind is another way of describing imaginations focused on God. It's a mind that is entwined with the mind of Christ. We imagine God's presence and praise Him, talk with Him and listen to Him. It's another way of saying that we worship Him. Worship is the greatest form of intimacy with God because He's in our heart. We are in communion with Him every day. The result of that intimacy is perfect peace.

We need to be in constant worship of God—worship of who He is and what He has done and will do for us. Worship needs to be integrated into our behavior, our family, our work, into all of life. It's not an external action—going to a church service once a week to sing some songs and listen to a religious message. Instead, it's an internal, intense imagination of constant love, praise and thanksgiving. It's a daily communion with our Creator, Redeemer and Sustainer!

Those who know your name will trust in you,
for you, Lord have never forsaken those who seek you.
Psalm 9:10

In the Bible, many words are used to identify God and name Him. Each of them reveals a different aspect of the God with whom we walk every day. They help us gain a greater understanding of the eternal God with whom we have an intimate relationship. Here we find images of God that can guide our thoughts and help us worship Him. Here we see His promises unfold. In the following verses, let's examine some of these words and what they reveal about God.

. . . . . .

In the beginning **God** created the heavens and the earth.
Genesis 1:1

The Hebrew word for God here is **Elohim**, the Eternal Creator who always was and always will be. Elohim is the God of power who created all and controls all, yet remains separate from His creation, as an artist from a painting. Elohim is a plural noun in form but has a singular meaning. It speaks of God as many, though He is one, which indicates His triune nature. Our imagination of Elohim is the one who exists beyond the boundaries of time, who with His almighty power created everything.

. . . . . .

The **Lord God** made the earth and the heavens.
Genesis 2:4

Here we see the word Lord used with God, or **Jehovah-Elohim**. Jehovah is the great and incommunicable name of

God. When it is combined with Elohim, the name means a God not just of power, but of perfection, a finishing God. We imagine Jehovah-Elohim as the Self-Existent One who gives life to all beings.

. . . . . .

"I am **God Almighty**; walk before me and be blameless. I will confirm my covenant between me and you and will greatly increase your numbers."
Genesis 17:1-2

God uses *El Shaddai*—God All-Sufficient—when He establishes His covenant with Abraham. By using this name, God pledges that He will strengthen and satisfy His people. Abraham will be fruitful, but it will be fruit carefully tended and purified. God will strengthen His people as a father strengthens a child: by meeting their needs and chastening them for their own good. Then they will flourish. Through Him they will be strong. Imagine El Shaddai as our strength, our source of comfort, our nourishment, our confidence and our satisfaction. He is All-Sufficient. We need nothing more.

. . . . . .

So Abraham called that place *The Lord Will Provide*. And to this day it is said, "On the mountain of the Lord it will be provided."
Genesis 22:14

The Lord who will provide is *Jehovah-Jireh*. Following God's command, Abraham had taken Isaac into the mountains to kill him as a sacrifice to God. Abraham had been faithful to God. He had given up all that God had asked—his country and kindred, his nephew Lot, his plans for his son Ishmael, and now his son Isaac. He built the altar, tied up Isaac and placed him on the wood. As he pulled out his knife to kill his son, an angel intervened and saved Isaac. God provided another sacrifice that day, a ram that had been caught in some bushes. And He later provided another sacrifice, His only son, who died for all our sins. Imagine God as a father, providing His son as a sacrifice for each of us.

"I am the **Lord**, who heals you."
Exodus 15:26

Jehovah-Rapha not only offers physical healing, but the healing of our souls. Jesus explains salvation in Matthew 9:12 when He says, "It is not the healthy who need a doctor, but the sick." Our souls are sick until we find satisfaction in Him. In the Christian life, He continues to be the Great Physician, so when we stray from a perfect vision of Him and our thoughts no longer reflect Him, we must come to Him for renewed healing. If we do not, the sickness in our soul will weaken, deform and destroy us. But God is faithful, and He promises to heal us. He brings us back to Himself, heals our soul and fills us with His satisfaction. Let this fill our imaginations.

. . . .

Moses built an altar and called it **The Lord is my Banner**.
Exodus 17:15

Soldiers on the battlefield usually have a flag or banner. The banner shows them which way to go in the heat of battle, and it gives them a symbol around which they rally. It becomes a source of pride, identity and inspiration. *Jehovah-Nissi* was the banner for the Israelites. And Isaiah describes Jesus as the banner for all of us. "In that day the Root of Jesse will stand as a banner for the peoples; the nations will rally to him, and his place of rest will be glorious" (Isaiah 11:10). The Lord is our Banner, our inspiration, our encouragement, our symbol and our guide.

. . . .

So Gideon built an altar to the Lord there and called it
The Lord is Peace.
Judges 6:24

Gideon felt little internal peace. God had called him to deliver the Israelites from the oppressive rule of the Midianites. Gideon didn't want the job. He didn't think he was up to the task, and he didn't have much faith that God would give him victory. Finally, he asked for a sign. He prepared an offering of meat and bread. Fire consumed it. Then Gideon understood God's calling. His heart was at peace.

Our heart can find the same peace of *Jehovah-Shalom* when we remember He is calling us. He will give us the tools we need to fulfill His calling. He is our peace in all circumstances. He is the ultimate image of peace.

. . . . . .

This is the name by which he will be called:
The Lord Our Righteousness.
Jeremiah 23:6

In this prophecy, Jeremiah explains that the Messiah will be *Jehovah-Tsidkenu*, which means the Lord, our righteousness, in Hebrew. Through His death on the cross, He is the One through whom we obtain righteousness. He is the Lord, who makes us right with God. He is our Savior, because His death on the cross gives us His righteousness in exchange for our sins.

. . . . . .

And the name of the city from that time on will be:
THE LORD IS THERE.
Ezekiel 48:35

Jehovah-Shammah reveals His abiding presence with His people. God tells Moses, "My Presence will go with you" (Exodus 33:14). David writes, "You will fill me with joy in your presence" (Psalm 16:11). Jesus promises, "And surely I am with you always, to the very end of the age" (Matthew 28:20). There is no greater comfort and satisfaction than to know that He is always with us.

. . . . . .

The Lord Almighty—he is the King of glory.
Psalm 24:10

Jehovah-Sabaoth, the Lord Almighty, is the Lord of Hosts. The word hosts has a special reference to service or warfare. Hosts is related to heavenly bodies (Genesis 2:1, Nehemiah 9:6, Isaiah 40:26) and angels (Luke 2:13). As Jehovah-Sabaoth, God is able to make His power known. He can marshal all the hosts to fulfill His purposes and to help His people. We find confidence in this name, knowing that He is our help and our strength.

. . . .

> "Say to the Israelites, 'You must observe my Sabbaths.
> This will be a sign between me and you for the
> generations to come, so you may know that
> I am the **Lord**, who makes you holy.' "
> **Exodus 31:13**

Jehovah-M'kaddesh sets us apart as a holy people of His own for His service. It is the Lord who sanctifies us and makes us holy. We cannot achieve such a standard on our own. "But you were washed, you were sanctified, you were justified in the name of the Lord Jesus Christ and by the Spirit of our God" (I Corinthians 6:11). His blood sets us apart; His blood makes us holy; His blood distinguishes us.

. . . .

> Come, let us bow down in worship,
> let us kneel before the **Lord our Maker**;
> for he is our God
> and we are the people of his pasture,
> the flock under his care.
> **Psalm 95:6-7**

We have a personal relationship with *Jehovah-Oseenu*, the Lord our Maker. He made each of us, and as our personal creator He has a right to us. Others may kneel down and worship gods and idols of their own making, but our God made us. We worship Him because He gives us life, and He preserves and protects us every day.

. . . .

> How awesome is the **Lord Most High,**
> the great King over all the earth!
> **Psalm 47:2**

God Most High, *El Elyon*, is the creator and ruler of earth. He is the rightful owner and Lord over all the creatures because He made them. What a wonderful image of God as the highest. When we belong to Him, He will protect us. He is the greatest King and Highest Lord.

. . . . . .

In these verses, we have seen God as our eternal and personal Creator, the One who gives us life, heals us, meets all our needs and gives us peace. He is always with us. He is our righteousness; He sanctifies us and makes us holy. Each of us can focus our thoughts and imaginations on these promises of God. We can know, in our head and in our heart, that He is deeply committed and involved with each of us. He has promised it through the names He uses.

In the Old Testament, God is our Creator who made us. We bow before Him and revere Him. He saves us and protects us. He is transcendent, above us. He is eternal, unchangeable and without limits. He is independent and self-existent. God is infinitely greater than all His creatures and infinite in holiness. God's transcendence is His greatness. These images reveal God's ability to create and sustain all the intricacies of the universe. They also reveal God as deeply and intimately concerned about each of us.

In the New Testament, God reveals Himself in a new way—He comes to man in flesh as the person of Jesus Christ. Christ is the path to the Father, our Creator, our Almighty, our Healer, our Banner, our constant Provider. He is immanent—near to us as our help and comfort. God becomes man to be our Redeemer. He is with us and we are in union with Him.

. . . . . .

So it is written: "The first man Adam became a living being"; the last Adam, a life-giving spirit.
I Corinthians 15:45

Jesus is the second Adam.
C.S. Lewis pointed out that in many myths of the ancient

world, gods came down and dwelt among men. For example, the Greeks believed that their gods lived with men and when men did foolish things, the gods began to despise them.

Christianity is different from these myths. The Lord Jesus is the great transcendent God who came down and lived among men and loved them to the degree of giving His life for their sins.

. . . .

God exalted him to his own right hand as Prince and Savior that he might give repentance and forgiveness of sins to Israel.
Acts 5:31

Jesus gives forgiveness to all who seek it in faith and repentance. That should be our overriding image of Him. Jesus' purpose is to bring us to Himself and then to the Father.

In our normal, human state we turn to the world. But Jesus provides our way for turning away from the world and turning to God. We find our place with Him, the one who is on the right hand of God.

Imagine calling on His name. Peter and Paul were able to accomplish amazing miracles in the name of Jesus. We can do the same. We can call on His name to cast out false imaginations. We can use His name to help us focus our thoughts, to bring the proper balance in our life. As Jesus brought everything under total submission to His Father, so we must bring everything under total submission to God—in the name of Jesus Christ.

Jesus has the power to change our life at this very moment—the power of peace, the power of wisdom, knowledge and discernment. Jesus is the key to our eternal relationship with God.

Remember, our imaginations today shape our eternity. Every day we need to begin with a fresh commitment to our relationship. Every day we need to focus our imaginations on finding satisfaction in Christ. Every day we need to renew our communion with the Lord. Every day we need to worship Him.

I delight greatly in the Lord;
my soul rejoices in my God.
For he has clothed me with garments of salvation
and arrayed me in a robe of righteousness.
Isaiah 61:10

This is the God with whom Enoch walked. This is the God in whom Paul rested and found contentment. This is the God who can clothe us in salvation and righteousness!

In our imaginations, we need to see ourselves in union with Him, knowing Him as we are known. Worshipping and walking with the Lord every day will transform our lives because it places Him at the center of our heart. Then we find true satisfaction. Hope, faith, peace and love are united in our souls as we become one with Christ and He becomes one with us. Our actions are guided by our love for Him and faith in His promises. True love, joy and peace are ours—now and for eternity!

C   H   A   P   T   E   R   1   2

Filled with Thanksgiving

TWO MEN WERE SITTING IN A CAFETERIA EATING LUNCH. AFTER A WHILE, THE FIRST SAID TO THE SECOND, "IS SOMETHING WRONG? DO YOU FEEL SICK?" THE SECOND SAID, "NO. WHAT DO YOU MEAN?" THE FIRST REPLIED, "OH, YOUR HEAD WAS DOWN." "I WAS JUST GIVING THANKS TO THE LORD," THE SECOND SAID. THE FIRST MAN RESPONDED, "YOU BELIEVE IN ALL THAT STUFF? I JUST START RIGHT IN WHEN I EAT." THE SECOND ANSWERED, "I UNDERSTAND WHAT YOU MEAN. MY DOG DOES THE SAME THING."

So often we can be just like dogs—jumping in without thanking God for all His blessings in our life. At times we begin to think we can take the credit for our house, our car, our family. But God has provided it all. We need to be thankful for our daily actions and activities and health, our love, our work, our ability to laugh. That imagination of thanksgiving is essential to a life of genuine worship.

Communion with God is real and meaningful when we are thankful to God. We walk with God genuinely when we appreciate His majesty, His person in Christ, the joy of living in His heart and the promise of being engulfed with Him forever.

A basic element of our relationship is a state of thanksgiving—a thanksgiving frenzy—that comes from every inch of our body as we go to work, perform household chores, get up in the morning and go to bed at night.

We need to live in a state of constant thanksgiving.

Give thanks in all circumstances, for this is God's will for
you in Christ Jesus.
I Thessalonians 5:18

Always giving thanks to God the Father for everything,
in the name of our Lord Jesus Christ.
Ephesians 5:20

A thankful spirit motivates our faith, our love, our
surrender to God. When we are truly thankful, it's because
we realize who God is and how sinful we are.

Joel Fish, a sports psychologist, says we must develop a
friendly, thankful mind when we participate in sports activities. Many golfers crack their clubs, slam clubs into the
ground and even throw clubs when they're frustrated about
their game. Those golfers haven't developed a thankful attitude about the game. When golf is played with thanksgiving,
joy and exuberance, performance excels.

During long races, when I'd run 24 to 30 hours, I didn't
think about myself. I didn't concentrate on the aches and
pains, the course ahead or how I'd performed to that point. I
didn't look down, I didn't look back and I didn't even look
ahead. I looked up. I quoted Scriptures, I sang songs praising
God, and I was thankful for the opportunity to be in the race
and for the ability He had given me to participate.

When I concentrated on being thankful, I didn't have
time and energy to notice the aches and pains that cropped
up during a race. When we turn our imaginations to thanking God in all the areas of our life, our mind is focused on
Him. It's more difficult for worldly imaginations and negative
attitudes to gain a foothold in our mind. A thankful spirit
helps us control all our imaginations.

Through Jesus, therefore, let us continually offer to God a
sacrifice of praise—the fruit of lips that confess his name.
Hebrews 13:15

But we must guard against thanking God only for our
possessions and ourselves. If we are thankful merely for pos-

sessions we have, we may be violating the pure beauty of the worship of thanksgiving. When we are expressing gratitude as a mere formality, or to make us feel good, or to take us away from our worries, we really are not worshipping God.

Our heart should overflow with thanksgiving for the person of Jesus Christ living in us. We should be filled with thanksgiving for knowing that we're saved. We need to rejoice that the Lord has taken our confessed sin and accepted our repentance. We need to live in a state of thanksgiving to God, seeing His work in our life every minute, every day. We can give thanks for His sovereignty, His love, His grace.

This ecstasy of thanksgiving comes when we realize that He is within us and will be with us forever. The greatest joy comes from being intertwined with the presence of God now and knowing that it will extend throughout eternity!

An Eternal Relationship

THINK BACK TO SOME RELATIONSHIPS YOU'VE HAD: WITH PARENTS, FRIENDS, SPOUSES AND CHILDREN. WHAT MAKES SOME RELATIONSHIPS SUCCESSFUL? WHY DO SOME STRUGGLE?

Robert J. Sternberg, a professor of psychology and education at Yale University, says a relationship is built on passion, intimacy and commitment. He says these elements form a "love triangle" between two people.

These elements also apply to our relationship with God.

Passion

Do we seek God out of a sense of obligation? Or do we search after Him as a deer pants after the brook?

Here's how one Psalm describes longing for God:

As the deer pants for streams of water,
so my soul pants for you, O God.
My soul thirsts for God, for the living God.
Psalm 42:1-2

In Jesus' day there was a pool of water in Bethesda believed to have healing powers. Jesus appeared to one man at the pool and asked, "Do you want to be healed?" He wanted to know the man's desire. Did he truly desire to be healed? Or was he there because others had told him to go there? What was his inner desire?

Christ wants to know the truth in each of us. Do we have a passion, a drive, a hope, a longing, a desire for intimacy with Christ? Even Paul, who wrote so eloquently about being content, said he wanted to know the Lord better and better.

Being married to Christ gives us a new focus, a new orientation, a new desire. In our new imaginations we passionately seek Christ. Now and for eternity. We're energized just thinking about the name of Jesus.

It's easy for us to become complacent. It's easy for us to become indifferent to God, imagining nothing rather than focusing on Him. It's easy to lose some of our passion for Christ.

Let us praise the Lord with our whole being. Let us hold on firmly to Him. Let us love Him, passionately and deeply, every day, with every thought and with every action.

Imagine your life when God permeates every feeling, every thought, every action. Imagine your life when your zeal for His presence fills your heart and mind. That emotion is from the wonder and worship of Him.

A speaker at a Promise Keepers meeting asked this question: Have you ever had a sexual relationship outside of marriage that was exotic and fascinating? Then he paused and said, "In your mind?" Certainly many of us have been tempted in our imaginations.

Now apply that to our relationship with God. Have you found worldly desires and fantasies creeping into your imaginations? Have you strayed from your longing for God?

As humans, we are frail and feeble beings. We struggle to keep our desire for God, but are lured by the material goods and attitudes of the world. We can lose sight of God's almighty power and wisdom. We fantasize about our own importance and our own abilities. We can think we have great knowledge. We can think we can control so many elements of our life.

But in truth, we know very little—and can control even less. We can never understand the simplest cell or the most grandiose parts of our universe. We have nothing without our Creator, our Redeemer, our Sustainer.

O God, you are my God,
earnestly I seek you;

my soul thirsts for you,
my body longs for you,
in a dry and weary land
where there is no water.
I have seen you in the sanctuary
and beheld your power and your glory.
Psalm 63:1-2

The writers of the Psalms knew that God set the universe in motion. And that He watches over each of us. Their response: to worship and love this Almighty God.

We can do no less. We need to deeply desire God, feeling His presence living within us and transforming our imaginations. We can be so deeply in love with Him that we don't fantasize about worldly possessions or goals. We find our perfect contentment in Him.

Now we must guard against that worship becoming a response of our own emotions. We can't generate the Lord's presence in us by being emotional. We need to let godly emotion radiate from us.

My soul yearns, even faints,
for the courts of the Lord;
my heart and my flesh cry out
for the living God.
Psalm 84:2

May each of us be lovers of God! May the Spirit quicken us, so that we have hope and belief in all the promises of God, and may His Word become real within our life. Let us cry out and seek an intimate relationship with Him, so that He is with us, He is in us and He is seen through us!

Intimacy
Another side of the triangle is intimacy, or "knowing." In both Hebrew and Greek, "to know" implies a relationship best seen in a very intimate marriage. We reveal our deepest thoughts, feelings and fears. We're willing to risk rejection as

we seek an intimate relationship. We also open ourselves up to another, letting them reveal themselves to us.

We have to know God. Not just know about Him, but know Him personally. We can know all about basketball superstar Michael Jordan, but we don't know him personally. It's only through a relationship that we get to know someone. We have to know God and know Him well.

Grace and peace be yours in abundance through the knowledge of God and of Jesus our Lord.
II Peter 1:2

Grow in the grace and knowledge of our Lord and Savior Jesus Christ.
II Peter 3:18

One of our greatest imaginations is that we have an intimate relationship with God. We are close to Him on a very personal basis. We must hold this image dearly.

God cries for our intimacy. He cries for us to know Him. He desires for us to understand Him and His inner workings, which have been and will forever be, and to know our place in the inner workings.

At the same time, we must be willing to open ourselves to Him. We have to let Him tear down the defensive, protective walls we build to prevent intimacy.

Search me, O God, and know my heart;
test me and know my anxious thoughts.
See if there is any offensive way in me,
and lead me in the way everlasting.
Psalm 139:23-24

The Psalmist invites God to search his heart, to probe the very depths of his imaginations. He gives God complete access. Are we willing to do that? Or are we afraid to let God into our heart completely?

We should be willing to share such perfect intimacy

with our Creator. He already knows us completely. We're not really hiding anything from Him anyway. But when we invite Him to search our thoughts, it's an invitation to share our weaknesses with Him. It reveals our attitude of surrender to Him.

We give ourselves completely—all our doubts and fears, all our negative imaginations and thoughts, all our sin. We're asking God to examine our thoughts and lead us back to faith, to strengthen our faith.

To be led in the everlasting way of God we must unburden all our sins. We must allow ourselves to be engulfed in His eternity.

> The Lord said to Moses, "Tell Aaron and his sons, 'This is how you are to bless the Israelites. Say to them:
> " ' "The Lord bless you and keep you;
> the Lord make his face shine upon you
> and be gracious to you;
> the Lord turn his face toward you and give you peace." '
> So they will put my name on the Israelites,
> and I will bless them."
> **Numbers 6:22-27**

We seek the imaginations of God's blessings as each of us looks to Him. May we know His love. May we be intimate with Him. May His presence determine our ways and our steps. God promises He will bless His people. He gives His blessing to those who love Him.

Commitment

How do we imagine ourselves? Do you see yourself as a person who can trust God, as a person who can have a relationship with God, as a person who is so committed to God that no sin can draw you away?

The story of Samson warns us what can happen when we aren't fully committed to God. His example warns us not to seek satisfaction outside God's provision, when our heart is inclined to the things of the world.

Samson had been dedicated by his parents to be a Nazirite, set aside to be faithful to God. He was special to God. "He will begin the deliverance of Israel from the hands of the Philistines" (Judges 13:5). Samson, a man of extraordinary strength, led Israel for 20 years.

But Samson was a flawed leader. As a young man, he married a Philistine woman, setting off a chain of events that led to violence and the death of his wife. While in Gaza years later, he slept with a prostitute, giving the Philistines a chance to trap and kill him. He managed to escape in the middle of the night with his life.

Then he met Delilah. Samson hadn't learned from his previous encounters, and he fell into the same snare. He loved Delilah. But she betrayed him to the Philistines. She pleaded with him until he revealed the source of his great strength—hair that had never been cut.

> "No razor has ever been used on my head," he said, "because I have been a Nazirite set apart to God since birth. If my head were shaved, my strength would leave me, and I would become as weak as any other man."
> **Judges 16:17**

After he fell asleep, she summoned someone to cut his hair and delivered a weakened Samson to the rulers of the Philistines. He was now their prisoner. And he would die as their prisoner, but not before he could demonstrate once again the power of the Lord.

While a prisoner, Samson's hair began to grow again. After a while, the Philistines summoned him to perform during a celebration at the temple of Dagon, the Philistines' false god.

> Then Samson reached toward the two central pillars on which the temple stood. Bracing himself against them, his right hand on the one and his left hand on the other, Samson said, "Let me die with the Philistines!" Then he pushed with all his might, and down came the temple

on the rulers and all the people in it.
Judges 16:29-30

Samson's earthly appetites led to his downfall. Yet he was a man of mighty faith in God, who called upon Him in the darkest moments. He renewed his commitment to the Lord. He remembered the true source of strength and satisfaction.

What about us? We may have all the passion and knowledge, but do we have the commitment to stay in a relationship with the person of Jesus Christ?

Commitment is essential in all relationships. Members in a business partnership are obliged to fulfill their obligations through a contract. Marriage partners pledge to remain committed to each other. Sometimes these commitments break down. Business people sue each other when contracts are broken. Spouses may divorce because one or the other wants to forget their commitment.

> One thing I ask of the Lord,
> this is what I seek:
> that I may dwell in the house of the Lord
> all the days of my life,
> to gaze upon the beauty of the Lord
> and to seek him in his temple.
> **Psalm 27:4**

Every day we need to dwell in the house of the Lord, embracing the Lord Jesus Christ. We must renew our commitment to think as God thinks. We need to have His eternal perspective, His holy attitude, His pure love.

Union with Christ

> You have made known to me the path of life;
> you will fill me with joy in your presence,
> with eternal pleasures at your right hand.
> **Psalm 16:11**

Our life as followers of Christ is where the glory of the Lord is revealed. Our part is to come close to Him, to walk along His path of life. Our whole purpose is to talk with Him in His language through prayer. We live in a state of eternal life as the Holy Spirit lives within us.

Our whole being seeks to unite with Him as one in our mind so we think with Him—we think as He thinks. That's what life is all about. It's to live in the aura, the glow, the excitement of being with the Lord. He will fill us with joy, and we will experience His eternal pleasures!

Where are we putting our investments? The most important investment we will ever make is determining how we think. Let us commit ourselves to uniting with the heart and mind of God. Let us invest in our eternal relationship with Him!

Soil Testing

I WANT TO ASK YOU A QUESTION. IF YOU WERE TO THINK OF YOURSELF AS SOIL, WHAT KIND WOULD YOU BE? ARE YOU WELL-WORN, LIKE A ROAD, INTO A GROOVE? DO YOU AVOID CHANGE, REJECTING NEW IDEAS AND APPROACHES?

Maybe you would consider yourself to be tough, rocky soil. You're always looking out for Number One. You're open to some new ideas, but they don't last. They don't get a chance to take root in your life.

Or are you open to all kinds of ideas and changes? They seem to sprout up like weeds. And then you find yourself easily distracted.

Then there's the kind of dirt gardeners love. It's full of nutrients, able to grow any flower or fruit. That's a person who can separate good ideas from bad ones, and be productive in his daily life.

Jesus used this analogy in a parable about whether we let godly thoughts into our life.

> A farmer went out to sow his seed. As he was scattering the seed, some fell along the path, and the birds came and ate it up. Some fell on rocky places, where it did not have much soil. It sprang up quickly, because the soil was shallow. But when the sun came up, the plants were scorched, and they withered because they had no root. Other seed fell among thorns, which grew up and choked the plants. Still other seed fell on good soil, where it produced a crop—a hundred, sixty or thirty times what was sown.
> **Matthew 13:3-8**

Do you see yourself in the story? Here's how Jesus explains the types of soil and the growth of God's seeds of true imaginations.

> When anyone hears the message about the kingdom and does not understand it, the evil one comes and snatches away what was sown in his heart. This is the seed sown along the path. The one who received the seed that fell on rocky places is the man who hears the word and at once receives it with joy. But since he has no root, he lasts only a short time. When trouble or persecution comes because of the word, he quickly falls away. The one who received the seed that fell among the thorns is the man who hears the word, but the worries of this life and the deceitfulness of wealth choke it, making it unfruitful. But the one who received the seed that fell on good soil is the man who hears the word and understands it. He produces a crop, yielding a hundred, sixty or thirty times what was sown.
> **Matthew 13:19-23**

The soil shows how we react to the Word of the Lord. The soils are all different, just as we are all different. What kept the seed from taking solid root was the condition of the soil. What keeps us from letting Christ take hold of our life is the condition of our heart and mind.

Sometimes we're hard ground or rocky places. Maybe a family member said something that made us callous. Maybe we don't feel accepted in society, so we don't want to accept anything else. Maybe we've had a negative experience with a church. Any of these events create negative thoughts, vain imaginations, that keep our heart locked up and unwilling to hear the Word of God.

Sometimes there are thorns in our life. We let the cares and desires of this world interfere with the Word of God trying to grow in us. We doubt God because we want worldly goods, and we think we can get them by our own power. We're anxious and fearful; we don't allow God to have a real relationship with us.

If we plant the garden and don't cultivate it, weeds grow. We can have Christ planted in our heart, but we must be cultivated so worldly imaginations don't destroy us.

Now let's look at what happens with the positive imaginations, when the seeds of God's Word land in the good soil. The seeds, His Word, change us. The imaginations of Christ fill our mind. We praise Him so much and are so thankful to Him that the diamonds associated with the crown of His majesty pierce our hard soil, our heart, our skin, our mind.

If we expect any kind of soil to produce fruit, it needs to be plowed. In the same way, we need to break up the soil of our mind and let God sow His Word in it.

The prophet Jeremiah directed the Israelites to do this:

This is what the Lord says to the men of
Judah and to Jerusalem:
  "Break up your unplowed ground
  and do not sow among thorns."
Jeremiah 4:3

We cannot let the soil of our mind be preoccupied with the world. Our life cannot be filled with positive imaginations of Christ until we get rid of our earthly way of thinking and are reborn spiritually with Him.

We must search our heart and pull out all the weeds the world has sown—the anger, the bitterness, the greed and, most of all, the selfishness. We need to let God take away all the hardness and resentments of our heart. We must be abandoned to God—and to Him alone.

Sow for yourselves righteousness,
reap the fruit of unfailing love,
and break up your unplowed ground;
for it is time to seek the Lord.
Hosea 10:12

Seeds don't always grow. Their development depends on the soil. As humans, we have a choice about our development. It's up to us. We determine whether we're going to receive His Word, His seed. He touches our heart. Do we respond to Him with complete surrender, seeking to fill our life with His thoughts?

Remember, the imaginations of our mind are what we become. Do we choose negative, earthly thoughts, or do we choose the complete peace, joy and thankfulness of the everlasting God?

React or Respond?

WHEN WE GIVE MEDICINES TO OUR PATIENTS, THEY EITHER REACT TO THEM OR THEY RESPOND TO THEM. REACTION IS BAD. RESPONSE IS GOOD. IT'S SIMILAR TO THE WAY WE HANDLE LIFE'S CIRCUMSTANCES. WE CAN REACT IN NEGATIVE AND HARMFUL WAYS OR WE CAN RESPOND IN A GODLY WAY. OUR SENSE OF SATISFACTION DETERMINES WHETHER WE REACT OR RESPOND.

Imagine someone insults you. Do you react or respond?

A gentle answer turns away wrath,
but a harsh word stirs up anger.
Proverbs 15:1

A gentle answer comes from positive imaginations, a loving attitude, thinking like Christ. A harsh word comes from negative imaginations, a worldly view in which we put ourselves first and are quick to judge and condemn others.

For example, when people invest in the stock market, they have imaginations of money. Those imaginations can be good or bad. They can imagine how they'll use money to serve God and help others. Or they can imagine how successful they'll be if they have more money. Then they quit thinking of God.

The complex life of King David is full of examples we can follow and lessons we can apply to our own life. He demonstrated over and over again the rich blessings of godly imaginations and the pain and destruction caused by worldly thoughts.

David was a very special person to God. "I have found David son of Jesse a man after my own heart," God said of him (Acts 13:22).

As a boy, David was anointed to be king of Israel. As king, he was a mighty military commander and powerful leader. He accomplished great deeds in the name of the Lord; he returned the Ark of the Covenant to the people of Israel. He was a person of action, author of beautiful poetry, a loyal friend and a judicious ruler and leader.

God loved David so much that He made a covenant with him.

> Your house and your kingdom will endure forever before me; your throne will be established forever.
> **II Samuel 7:16**

God honored David by pledging that Jesus would be his descendant. From the house and family of David would come the Savior of the world.

But David also had some grievous failings. He sinned greatly before the Lord and he repented deeply. His life shows us that no one lives in perfect obedience to the law. It also shows us how much God desires a relationship with each of us.

Let's look at two examples in David's life of how thoughts affect actions and change our life.

The Israelites were at war with the Philistines. David's older brothers went off to battle, while David, who was still a boy, stayed home to look after the family's sheep.

David's father, Jesse, sent David to the battlefield with provisions for his brothers and other troops. When he reached the Israelite camp, he had his first encounter with Goliath, the giant warrior. He heard Goliath taunt the Israelites, and he saw the Israelites cower.

David was outraged that Goliath could insult the people of God in such a way. And he was equally outraged that the "armies of the living God" would run (I Samuel 17:26). The

Israelites had imaginations of fear and doubt. David would not be influenced by such thinking. His faith would not be shaken, even by a 9-foot warrior. David found his way to Saul, the king and commander of the Israelites. "Let no one lose heart on account of this Philistine; your servant will go and fight him" (I Samuel 17:32).

To Saul, this was unthinkable. David was a boy; Goliath a seasoned soldier. But David knew he had one additional factor in his favor: faith in God. He knew the God who kept him safe as he defended sheep from lions and bears would keep him safe in battle against Goliath. So Saul agreed to let David fight.

Goliath was insulted that the Israelites would send an inexperienced boy into battle. David saw Goliath, with all his impressive armor, shield and sword. His courage didn't waver. He didn't run. His trust in God was unshakable. He had faith in God's promises.

> You come against me with sword and spear and javelin, but I come against you in the name of the Lord Almighty, the God of the armies of Israel, whom you have defied. This day the Lord will hand you over to me, and I'll strike you down and cut off your head...and the whole world will know that there is a God in Israel. All those gathered here will know that it is not by sword or spear that the Lord saves; for the battle is the Lord's, and he will give all of you into our hands.
> **I Samuel 17:45-47**

David knew that mere weapons were no match for the Almighty God. His thoughts were focused on the power of God; no earthly show of strength could weaken his faith.

> So David triumphed over the Philistine with a sling and a stone; without a sword in his hand he struck down the Philistine and killed him.
> **I Samuel 17:50**

David's imaginations of faith guided his actions. He believed God would protect him and give him the victory. So he felt bold in battle. His encounter was one of courage because he trusted in God. Years later, after David had become a mighty king, we encounter another kind of imagination. The book of II Samuel tells us about David's great struggle with sin.

In one military campaign, David stayed in Jerusalem while the troops went off to war. Late at night, he saw a beautiful woman bathing, and found out she was Bathsheba, wife of Uriah.

Already, David was in trouble. He wasn't with his troops, leading his army in battle for the Lord. He was neglecting his business, and therefore was more susceptible to temptation. And even though he knew Bathsheba was married, that fact didn't keep him from acting on his desires.

> Then David sent messengers to get her. She came to him, and he slept with her.
> **II Samuel 11:4**

David fell further and further into a web of sin and deceit. When Bathsheba discovered she was pregnant, David sent for her husband, hoping to trick everyone into thinking Uriah was the baby's father. That didn't work. Uriah refused to sleep with his wife while his troops were far away in battle. Unlike David, he focused his imaginations on the task at hand: success in battle.

David hatched another plan.

> In the morning David wrote a letter to Joab and sent it with Uriah. In it he wrote, "Put Uriah in the front line where the fighting is fiercest. Then withdraw from him so he will be struck down and die."
> **II Samuel 11:14-15**

First he committed adultery, then murder. After Uriah's death, David married Bathsheba, but the matter didn't end there. God knew the truth.

In an encounter with the prophet Nathan, David finally understood the deep sorrow he had brought upon God and the pain he had brought to everyone involved in the deception.

> Then David said to Nathan, "I have sinned against the Lord."
>
> Nathan replied, "The Lord has taken away your sin. You are not going to die. But because by doing this you have made the enemies of the Lord show utter contempt, the son born to you will die."
> **II Samuel 12:13-14**

David had let a mindset of selfishness, greed and lust influence his actions.

As king, he had everything he could ever want, yet he still wanted something more—Bathsheba. He was no longer satisfied in the promises of God.

In his selfishness, he lost his mindset of faith in God, and he brought about pain, suffering and death. The child did indeed die. But God forgave David. And He blessed David and Bathsheba with another son, Solomon, who became one of the wisest men of the Bible.

These two stories show how David's actions were influenced by his affections, his imaginations. When he looked to God, he succeeded; when he looked inward, at his own selfish needs, he failed.

What do we learn from David's experiences? In our decisions and our actions, our mindset is critical. Now, we may not face physical giants such as Goliath in our daily life. But we do face choices every day about how we focus our mind and how we act.

Few of us will destroy kingdoms because of our thoughts, but families and friends can suffer because of the actions that result from vain imaginations.

The meditations and imaginations of our mind determine our actions. Shall we become a king for the Lord or shall we disrupt our life because of vain imaginations?

Those who live in accordance with the Spirit have their minds set on what the Spirit desires...the mind controlled by the Spirit is life and peace.
Romans 8:5, 6

Paul tells us to focus on Christ. And when we think on Him, we will respond to life's circumstances with godly imaginations. May His peace and love guide our actions in every situation. Amen!

The Battle

LIKE DAVID, WE ARE UNDER ATTACK EVERY DAY BY WORLDLY IMAGINATIONS. WHY DO WE IMAGINE OURSELVES DOING THINGS THAT ARE WRONG RATHER THAN IMAGINE OURSELVES PRAYING? WHY DO WE SEEK AFTER MATERIAL POSSESSIONS RATHER THAN BEING WITH OUR FAMILIES, SERVING GOD, SHARING THE GOSPEL? WHY CAN'T WE KEEP OUR THOUGHTS FOCUSED ON THE LORD?

A man I know runs a help line for young people in distress. He said the biggest problem faced by people seeking his help is the constant warring between worldly goals and godly ones.

All of us are under assault. We're constantly barraged by the goals of the world. The world says it's OK to focus on ourselves first, it's OK to acquire more goods and possessions, it's OK to cheat, steal and lie if it helps us get what we want. This message is repeated every day by television, the Internet, Madison Avenue advertising and sometimes even by friends and family.

Under such an assault, even the strongest of us can succumb to worldly imaginations. It only makes sense. If we play in a garbage pile, we're going to get dirty. If we allow garbage—worldly thoughts and vain imaginations—to fill our minds, we will be worldly.

Earthly desires are harmful; they destroy us and those around us.

But we cannot give up when our thoughts are under attack. We cannot let worldly thoughts win. This is not a minor skirmish that we can ignore. If we let the world win, we are headed for eternity without Christ!

> When tempted, no one should say, "God is tempting me." For God cannot be tempted by evil, nor does he tempt anyone; but each one is tempted when, by his own evil desire, he is dragged away and enticed. Then, after desire has conceived, it gives birth to sin; and sin, when it is full-grown, gives birth to death.
> **James 1:13-15**

This is a battle for our eternal life that pits us against the full force of Satan.

> For our struggle is not against flesh and blood, but against the rulers, against the authorities, against the powers of this dark world and against the spiritual forces of evil in the heavenly realms.
> **Ephesians 6:12**

Why would Satan care what kinds of thoughts fill our mind? Why does he continually tempt us? Because he knows that *we are what we think.*

This battle for our mind is the most important fight of our life because the choices we make, influenced by our thoughts and imaginations, determine our eternal destiny. Who will we let win the war—Satan or the Almighty God?

Our goal is to think as God thinks, not to be controlled by worldly attitudes.

If we think about the world, we're going to be disappointed. If we think about God, we're going to be truly rewarded—now and for eternity. Yet our mind can be blinded by Satan's lies.

> The god of this age has blinded the minds of unbelievers, so that they cannot see the light of the gospel of the glory of Christ, who is the image of God.
> **II Corinthians 4:4**

Satan comes in many conduits and channels. He may be dressed well, culturally accepted and advertised beautifully, but he's still Satan. He will attack each of us differently, because he knows our individual weaknesses. But he seeks the same result in each of us. He wants to blind us to the glory of Christ.

He lures us away from the person of Jesus Christ gently at first, but before long we're tied up in his bonds of deception. Satan can convince us to doubt God as he did Adam and Eve. "Can you really believe God and what He says?"

As Satan lured Adam and Eve, he can do the same with us today and will do that tomorrow! It's difficult to avoid. We have to battle our own human nature.

Worldly thoughts can easily yank at us. "Come on, let's go have a good time." What we're really headed for is trouble. When our desires take us away from faith in God's promises, they become sin.

At times, all of us have used our imaginations in hurtful, selfish ways. We face a constant battle between the thoughts and desires of this world and the faith that leads to surrender to God and a transforming relationship with Christ.

All sins, all negative attitudes and harmful actions originate when we're lacking that transforming faith—when we don't believe the promises of God; when we don't live as though we believe in the promises of God; and when we let our selfishness take control of our thoughts and actions.

Everything that does not come from faith is sin.
Romans 14:23

Anything that is not of faith in the person of Jesus Christ is sin. Anything that is not of faith will lead to an aberration of peace, an aberration of joy and an aberration of love.

Sin is not against other people; it is against God. Sin is preferring the world to God. Sin is when we are not satisfied with God; we need the world to satisfy us.

Such behavior is the outgrowth of a deceitful heart, a heart not truly focused on the pure and perfect imaginations of God.

For out of the heart come evil thoughts, murder, adultery, sexual immorality, theft, false testimony, slander.
Matthew 15:19

The foundation for godly living is godly thinking. It's simple, but it's not easy.

We must guard against dwelling on the "maybe" of temptations. For example, maybe we're attracted to someone with whom we have a close friendship. And if the relationship isn't going right with a spouse, this other person seems even more attractive. Then we think about what "maybe" could happen.

We need to defeat these "maybes" with an emphatic "NO." We must bring these imaginations under control before they take on a life of their own. We should focus on seeking the Lord's face and His help to overcome and bring all these thoughts captive.

Fighting sin and fighting Satan is a continual process. Think about it as taking care of a yard. We can go out every day and pull the weeds out of our yard. But we don't pull all the root system, so the weeds keep growing back. So we get a gardening tool to dig out all the roots, and we get some weed killer to make sure we stop them.

And after a while, sure enough, the weeds are gone. But then we start getting moles in the yard. Now we have to find a way to destroy the moles.

This is how sin works in our life. We have to forcefully destroy it and constantly attack it. But we also have to make sure we put something else into our life to keep Satan away. We must let God's Holy Spirit and His Word fill our life. We must let our imaginations of loving and serving Him, and others, stir up holy desires and efforts. Otherwise selfish, sinful imaginations will continue to take root in our life and produce destructive thoughts and actions.

We've talked before about the need to surrender our selfishness and our pride. Paul uses strong language to warn us about the dangers of selfish desires and vain imaginations. He also tells us how to battle sin—finding satisfaction in the promises of God.

If anyone teaches false doctrines and does not agree to the sound instruction of our Lord Jesus Christ and to godly teaching, he is conceited and understands nothing. He has an unhealthy interest in controversies and quarrels about words that result in envy, strife, malicious talk, evil suspicions and constant friction between men of corrupt mind, who have been robbed of the truth and who think that godliness is a means to financial gain.

But godliness with contentment is great gain. For we brought nothing into the world, and we can take nothing out of it. But if we have food and clothing, we will be content with that. People who want to get rich fall into temptation and a trap and into many foolish and harmful desires that plunge men into ruin and destruction. For the love of money is a root of all kinds of evil. Some people, eager for money, have wandered from the faith and pierced themselves with many griefs.
I Timothy 6:3-10

Remember the story of Samson? He was totally committed to God for a while, but then he started looking for worldly satisfaction.

We can be like Samson, falling victim to sin when our earthly appetites lead us away from satisfaction in the Lord. We can succumb to the "Delilahs of the mind" because we aren't satisfied in our current circumstances. And like Samson, we can call upon the Lord and trust in Him for our strength. He will restore us when we seek His forgiveness.

What is our Delilah? We are covetous by nature. We want more and more. Advertising agencies tap into this desire, increasing the aroma of covetousness by suggesting we need bigger and better possessions.

Coveting, whether in the form of money, lust, careers or other idols of the world, draws us off the path of believing in the promises of God. It makes us believe we can be content with external possessions and goals. There is no lasting meaning in the idols of the world.

Some people struggle with being content in their physical needs. They can never have enough material possessions, no matter how much they own. They are lured by the false imagination that material goods offer complete comfort.

> Whoever loves money never has money enough;
> whoever loves wealth is never satisfied with his income.
> This too is meaningless.
> As goods increase,
> so do those who consume them.
> And what benefit are they to the owner
> except to feast his eyes on them?
> **Ecclesiastes 5:10-11**

I know others who battle the desire for contentment through money—the tangible measure of success in this world. J.P. Morgan was once asked, "How much money does it take to make people who work for you happy?" He said, "Oh, just a little bit more than they have."

Who of us hasn't wanted just a little more? Money is one of the greatest lures into false thinking because it shows we want man's power, not the power of the Almighty God. The desire to be rich, to buy human accomplishments, is a snare and a trap. It takes our focus off God's promise that He will provide. We don't see the danger until we're in it. Greed is a deadly vice. It kills and blots out God's presence within us.

> For the love of money is a root of all kinds of evil. Some people, eager for money, have wandered from the faith and pierced themselves with many griefs.
> **I Timothy 6:10**

Wealth is an attitude. The love of money is the sin, not money itself. The richest person is the one who can say, "I don't need anything more. I have a relationship with the living God."

Others face Delilahs at work. They may never be content in a job, and therefore move from job to job. And some let their desire for success at work interfere with their performance, their relationships with co-workers and, most of all, with their desire to do work that honors and glorifies God first.

> Therefore, my dear brothers, stand firm. Let nothing move
> you. Always give yourselves fully to the work of the Lord,
> because you know that your labor in the Lord is not in vain.
> **I Corinthians 15:58**

Our work needs to reflect our focus on God. We especially need to stand firm in the workplace, serving God and loving others.

Relationships pose a range of problems. I've seen marriages in which one spouse is seeking a "perfect" partner and therefore is never content. So that person strays from the marriage to seek perfection, and ends up destroying the relationship. We have to let imaginations of God transform us into people who are content in relationships with others. Each member is "the best significant other" when the other is satisfied with him or her, and him or her alone.

Jesus gives us the formula for right relationships.

> "Love the Lord your God with all your heart and with all
> your soul and with all your mind." This is the first and
> greatest commandment. And the second is like it:
> "Love your neighbor as yourself."
> **Matthew 22:37-39**

Another Delilah is the need for recognition from others. The Lord asks us to be content, to not seek awards and glory and praise from others. Striving for self-attained recognition takes us away from seeking the mind of Christ. When we seek to get our recognition from the world, we usually fail to get enough. We think we don't get the recognition we deserve. Or even if we get what we deserve, we want more. Instead, what we should seek is to be aligned with Christ, finding ourselves fulfilled by His love. His standard, not the praise of men, is what matters.

For it is not the one who commends himself who is approved, but the one whom the Lord commends.
II Corinthians 10:18

Some people crave excitement and adventure and will make reckless decisions based on their adventurous desires. I know doctors who make decisions in their profession just to create excitement. I know people who choose their business projects for the excitement the project generates. These choices aren't beneficial. They don't always help or serve others. The desire for excitement and adventure must be balanced with the desire to serve God. We find genuine excitement and adventure in our relationship with Him.

The Lord is my strength and my shield;
my heart trusts in him, and I am helped.
My heart leaps for joy
and I will give thanks to him in song.
Psalm 28:7

Our thoughts determine our destiny. God knows this. Satan knows this. Do we act as though we know it? Why do we choose to be half-filled by the material goods of this world rather than completely filled, and completely content, by the Lord God? Like a goalless child we make time pass in recreation, in ambition in our careers, in social activities and functions, in half-hearted relationships.

Our mind becomes filled with how we're going to fit everything in, and God gets squeezed into a corner of fleeting acknowledgment. How many times have we wanted money and the pleasures it pretends to buy, only to later regret that we've lost sight of God?

We damage ourselves and our relationship with Him when we chase Delilahs. Life in this world is full of tinsel, of fleeting diversions and thrills and entertainments that lure us away from God. And even though we may lose our focus on Him, we still feel the need to be content. So we seek satisfaction in various escapes—mystic escapes, moral escapes or material escapes.

There's an often-told story to illustrate this search.

A certain man grew up on a farm in a small town. He worked and plowed on this farm. But while he was on the farm he dreamed of one day searching the world looking for diamonds. To him, diamonds were the greatest symbol of riches, beauty and success in life. When he woke up in the morning, he thought of diamonds. When he plowed a field, he thought of mining for diamonds. When he went to bed at night, he had dreams of diamonds.

Eventually, he left his farm and his hometown and went out into the world. For 40 years he hunted around the globe for diamonds. He became an explorer and negotiator so he could start diamond mines in many obscure places. He became an inventor so he could devise new mining techniques. He became a scientist so he could determine the best places to search for diamonds. But he never reached his goal. He never uncovered diamonds.

He finally went back to his hometown. He was a broken man who was ready to spend his remaining years of life where he had started. But he had to reintroduce himself to the townspeople because he had changed so much during the years of searching for diamonds.

Upon his return he learned that the largest diamond ever mined was found on the farm he had once owned. He had sold the land for a pittance and now it was worth a fortune. His search for success had taken him around the world, and the one thing he had truly wanted was under his nose the whole time.

His search had been misdirected. In looking for earthly success, he found only disappointment. If he'd been content, appreciating what God had given him, he would have found earthly success, certainly, because the diamond was in his land the whole time. But he would have also found a richer satisfaction through the person of Jesus Christ.

How about us? Are we aware of the battle for our minds? Do we acknowledge the temptations of this world? Are we ready to fight worldly thoughts and surrender ourselves to God? Do we have a worldly view or an eternal perspective?

Do not love the world or anything in the world. If anyone loves the world, the love of the Father is not in him. For everything in the world—the cravings of sinful man, the lust of his eyes and the boasting of what he has and does—comes not from the Father but from the world. The world and its desires pass away, but the man who does the will of God lives forever.
I John 2:15-17

With faith in God, nothing can defeat us! We are walking in God and He is in us. We have His love, His power, His peace. We trust in His eternal provision. We can rest in His presence now and for eternity.

So often we know this in our heart, but our mind wars against it, creating confusion, distortion and anxiety. For example, we can have faith in our heart, but our mind becomes afraid. So we worry, we let ourselves be intimidated and lured by the attitudes and material goods of this world, we find ourselves in a sinful attitude—a breeding ground for selfishness and vain imaginations.

The god of this world has a plan to catch and snare those who have great potential in the kingdom of God. Will we be lured away by the lies of this god? Or will we let our mind be satisfied with the promises of God?

You were taught, with regard to your former way of life, to put off your old self, which is being corrupted by its deceitful desires; to be made new in the attitude of your minds; and to put on the new self, created to be like God in true righteousness and holiness.
Ephesians 4:22-24

We need to put on the new attitude of thanksgiving and worship. Then we will see eternity stretching out before us with the person of Jesus Christ.

Let us look no longer to the world for solutions and fulfillment; let us look to Christ. We will be engulfed in His presence forever! He will be our provider forever!

Making Our Choice

AT AGE 16 OUR LOOKS ARE DETERMINED BY WHAT WE'RE GIVEN. YET BY AGE 60 OUR LOOKS ARE DETERMINED MORE BY THE LIFESTYLE CHOICES WE'VE MADE. WE REALLY DO CHOOSE MOST OF THE EFFECTS ON OUR LIFE. WE CAN CHOOSE TO EXERCISE AND EAT RIGHT. OR WE CAN CHOOSE TO BE UNCONCERNED ABOUT OUR DIET AND WEIGHT. WE CAN CHOOSE TO ENJOY OUR WORK OR COMPLAIN ABOUT OUR WORK. WE CAN CHOOSE TO BE GENEROUS OR STINGY. WE CAN CHOOSE TO CRITICIZE OTHERS, OR WE CAN CHOOSE TO ENCOURAGE THEM. WE CAN CHOOSE TO BE INTROVERTS OR EXTROVERTS. WE CAN CHOOSE HAPPINESS. WE CAN CHOOSE SORROW.

Life is full of choices. The greatest choice of all is choosing what we'll think. We choose how we control our minds.

We are responsible for what we think and what we do with our thoughts. And we're responsible for the results of our thoughts. When we decide what we will allow to motivate us, we decide what kind of people we will be.

We choose whether to be positive or negative. We choose whether to be angry, violent, depressed or worried. We choose to either be constructive, using emotions that build us up, or to be negative, using emotions that damage us and those around us. We choose to be satisfied in God's promises or to be selfish, filled with worldly desires.

Most important, we choose either eternal life with Jesus Christ or eternity without Him. We choose whether to align ourselves, as Jonathan Edwards says, to God. When we choose God, we get our benefits, in Christian terms, as His blessings. We choose spiritual death or life everlasting in Christ. In the battle for our eternal life, which side do we choose?

> You adulterous people, don't you know that friendship with the world is hatred toward God? Anyone who chooses to be a friend to the world becomes an enemy of God.
> **James 4:4**

It's the greatest choice we face: Do we focus our thoughts on the world, or do we focus our thoughts on God? Do we fix our mind on Him? Or do we clutter our mind with false imaginations? Do we direct our thoughts according to worldly standards or do we seek the mind of Christ?

Elijah confronted King Ahab and the people of Israel about their choice.

King Ahab was one of the worst kings of Israel. The book of I Kings describes how Ahab set up the worship of Baal, a mock deity. His wife, Queen Jezebel, worshiped idols and witchcraft, and she was malicious and vicious.

Elijah, the great prophet, told the Israelites that God was displeased with them because they worshiped idols. He warned them that a drought would cover the land and punish them for their sins. Then God told Elijah to leave the region and directed the prophet to a safe place where God would provide for him. The Israelites, under the reign of Ahab, were on their own.

Sure enough, the drought came and famine was severe. Queen Jezebel persecuted the followers of God, killing many and forcing the remainder to go into hiding. Finally, God ordered Elijah to return to the region. "Go and present yourself to Ahab, and I will send rain on the land" (I Kings 18:1).

Elijah confronted Ahab and told him to "summon the people from all over Israel to meet me on Mount Carmel. And bring the four hundred and fifty prophets of Baal and the four hundred prophets of Asherah, who eat at Jezebel's table" (I Kings 18:19).

Ahab and the people gathered, expecting Elijah to bless them and pray for rain; but Elijah had other priorities.

> Elijah went before the people and said, "How long will you waver between two opinions? If the Lord is God, follow him; but if Baal is God, follow him."
>
> But the people said nothing.
> **I Kings 18:21**

The people were silent. They refused to take a stand about whom they would follow and how they would direct their thoughts. To this point, some had worshiped the Lord God and some had worshiped Baal. Even worse, sometimes they worshiped one and sometimes the other. Elijah knew that those who waver in their loyalty are not only unstable in their faith, they do not function well in the rest of their life.

Elijah proposed a test. Each side would prepare a sacrifice and call on the name of their God to light the fire around the sacrifice. The supporters of Baal had all the external advantages. Their camp included 450 prophets and the power of the king and his court. Elijah was just one man, alone in his faith in the Lord. The people agreed to the contest.

From morning to evening, the prophets of Baal called on their god. They danced, they shouted, they even cut themselves with swords to draw blood, trying to appease Baal. Nothing happened. "There was no response, no one answered, no one paid attention" (I Kings 18:29).

Then it was Elijah's turn. He built an altar with 12 stones, one for each tribe of Israel. He placed the wood around the altar and prepared the sacrifice. Then he did something amazing. He soaked the offering and the wood with water. Three times. There was no way on earth that the wood would catch fire.

> At the time of sacrifice, the prophet Elijah stepped forward and prayed: "O Lord, God of Abraham, Isaac and Israel, let it

be known today that you are God in Israel and that I am your servant and have done all these things at your command. Answer me, O Lord, answer me, so these people will know that you, O Lord, are God, and that you are turning their hearts back again."

Then the fire of the Lord fell and burned up the sacrifice, the wood, the stones and the soil, and also licked up the water in the trench.

When all the people saw this, they fell prostrate and cried, "The Lord, he is God! The Lord—he is God!"
I Kings 18:36-39

After such a powerful display, the people chose God. Today, we are faced with the same choice. Do we choose the fleeting pleasures that come from worshipping false gods? Or do we choose the living God, the mighty Jehovah who sends fire from heaven to show His power and might?

Jesus describes our situation this way:

No one can serve two masters. Either he will hate the one and love the other, or he will be devoted to the one and despise the other.
Matthew 6:24

We become spiritual warriors as we come to Christ. When we choose the eternal life of God, we choose sides. Even though we'll still be assaulted by the thoughts of this world, we must stay focused on Him.

So much of life tries to knock us down, knock us out of the ring, and knock us out of the fight. We must choose whether we get back up and keep going. Every day when we wake up we choose whether to love and serve God. We choose whether our imaginations of Him are positive, or whether we're going to destroy that day with negative imaginations and thoughts. Every day matters. Every day makes a difference.

Bill Anderson, a pastor in Clearwater, Fla., and I talk about how so many elements in life compete for our attention. Each one wants to be chosen. As a pastor, Bill has seen many people wrestle with the decision to choose Jesus Christ. He has seen them struggle to keep their mind and heart focused on God.

Sometimes we think we can have it all. We think we don't have to choose between God and the world. So we play along to get along.

In reality, this unfocused life is filled with great anxiety, stress and frustration. We lack the ability to concentrate on our work and to follow through on promises and commitments. We become inconsistent, indifferent and incompetent in all we try to accomplish. Being divided between the two is like having one foot in one boat and the other foot in another boat. We will be jerked apart and end up drowning.

God wants our total commitment—all of us or none of us. He doesn't want some attention from us when it's convenient, or only when we're in trouble. There is but one God, and He will meet our needs.

We will not choose imaginations focused on Christ if we have a worldly perspective. Leonardo da Vinci said, "Perspective is to art what a bridle is to a horse or a rudder to a boat."

What's our perspective? What's our rudder? What guides us? The eternal perspective will give us the ability to know where to go and how to control ourselves.

Let us have an imagination of anticipation: eternal life with Christ. An eternal life that begins the minute we surrender to Him, the minute we commit ourselves to Him in faith, the minute we accept His priceless grace. We are freed from all the concerns of the world, the affections of the world. We are not merely reformed, trying to improve what already is within us. Instead we are transformed. God has given us a glorious eternal life we can enjoy this day, this moment.

Let us imagine that eternal city, where there's perfect peace and complete joy, where we are in harmony with God and others. We have no worries, we have no fears. We have eternal life with our Creator, Redeemer and Sustainer. Richard Baxter, in his book *The Saints' Everlasting Rest*, exhorts us to take a walk in the New Jerusalem every day and enjoy the place Christ is preparing for us.

Let us imagine that city every day. May that vision guide us every day, so that our eternal life with Christ begins now. Then the focus of our imaginations is to always be "with Him," fully focused on the mind of Christ every day.

Have you made the choice about who you will follow? Have you decided what will motivate your thoughts? Have you decided what kind of person you will be?

Make that choice for Jesus Christ! Discover the eternal fountains of joy and peace, thanksgiving and hope, love and grace that He holds for you and for me. Jesus calls each of us to come to His cross and find forgiveness, and then to follow Him. I pray you hear His voice today.

Spiritual Conditioning

ONCE WE'VE BEEN QUICKENED BY THE HOLY SPIRIT, CAN WE SIT BACK AND RELAX? IS OUR LIFE GOING TO BE A PERFECT EXAMPLE OF SATISFACTION AND PEACE? IS THERE ANYTHING MORE WE NEED TO DO?

We have the mind of Jesus because we are being transformed by the Word and the Holy Spirit. We must refocus every day. We must reprogram our mind so that we are strong Christians.

The secret to keeping the true imaginations of God constantly in our heart is to daily reapply our mind to our relationship with Him.

Therefore, prepare your minds for action.
1 Peter 1:13

Be self-controlled and alert. Your enemy the devil prowls around like a roaring lion looking for someone to devour.
1 Peter 5:8

In sports, training makes an athlete stronger. If we're committed to a sport, we train for it and receive rewards for our performance. If we're committed to our profession, we get our rewards from it. If we're committed to the world, we get blessings from the world.

Spiritual conditioning is just as vital. We become couch potatoes spiritually unless we train our mind to focus on God. If we're committed to Him, we get our blessings from God's presence working through us.

Let us fix our eyes on Jesus, the author and perfector of
our faith, who for the joy set before him endured the
cross, scorning its shame, and sat down at the right hand of
the throne of God.
Hebrews 12:2

We need to fix our eyes on Jesus. As an athlete conditions
his body, we must condition all the elements of our minds—
our daydreams and fantasies, expectations, attitudes,
thoughts, meditations, images, vision—to find satisfaction in
God's promises. The only way to control those imaginations
is to think of God in everything we do. We must be with Him
and enjoy Him in everything!

We need to think of Christ not only as the Savior who
saved us once through repentance, but we must think of Him
as continually saving us as we constantly wash our minds and
wash our thoughts. We must live in a state of constantly asking God to forgive our rebellious nature.

We demolish arguments and every pretension that sets
itself up against the knowledge of God, and we take captive
every thought to make it obedient to Christ.
II Corinthians 10:5

With all our might, we have to take our thoughts captive
and diligently seek the transformation of our mind. We
should seek for His thoughts to become our thoughts, His will
to become our will and His heart to become our heart.

To build a fortress, the builder places one brick at a time.
Few things are accomplished immediately. In our physical
development, our mental development, our athletic development and our spiritual development we must take one area
and develop a little bit each day.

All of us are responsible for our thoughts, whether they
are based in the mind of Christ or directed by the desires of
this world. Since God has given us the responsibility for our
thoughts, He has given us the tools to control and direct
them. We are responsible for the choices we make about how
we act on our thoughts.

We cannot be spiritual couch potatoes. We must develop thought processes that focus on God and our relationship with Him in His eternal kingdom. Then our actions will be based on our eternal imaginations of Him, not on the false promises of this world.

Above all else, guard your heart,
for it is the wellspring of life.
Proverbs 4:23

This verse reminds us that we're responsible for our imaginations, which affect all areas of our life. Our imaginations are the spring from which all the issues and actions of our life flow. It's essential that we guard our thoughts, keeping faithful, fervent and focused on the Word of God.

Our success is based not on a situation, but on our disposition.

Our response can never be based on outward circumstances, but on our inner attitude and how well we condition our minds.

Let's look at some of the tools we can use to condition our minds, such as Bible study and prayer, discipline and setting priorities.

Think First or Act First?

Now, if we control our thoughts, can we think ourselves into acting as Christ would? Or is the reverse true? Do our Christ-like actions help us take on the mind of Christ?

Many people would say it's certainly easier to act ourselves into godly thoughts, because the exercises of godly actions build up the muscles of godly thought. We act ourselves into our mindset.

C.S. Lewis said that people turn into what they try to be. So, if we put our efforts into being full of joy, we become joyful.

There's a story told about a prince who was courting a woman. He wasn't very good looking, so he wore a mask of a handsome man to try and win the affections of the woman. When he finally took off the mask he was truly handsome.

Like that mask, our actions can mold our feelings. We must create the action of walking out in faith, walking out in love.

The action will create the feeling. We become very much like the roles we play. We do it in sports, we do it in our profession and we do it in relationships.

The great pitcher Nolan Ryan said that a person can't control his mind until he controls his body. I think he was saying that we must be disciplined and balanced in all areas. It's important that we control not only our body, but more importantly our mind and our thoughts.

It doesn't matter whether thoughts or actions come first. But it is essential that the two be balanced.

We can get pulled into a mindset, even if we go to church, that our actions are more important than our thoughts and attitudes. We can start to believe that if we give enough money to a church, or join enough committees, or do enough work in the name of the church, that our actions are sufficient. In other words, we start to believe in the church, not in the person of Jesus Christ.

We have to guard against letting religion and tradition take the place of Jesus. The goal is not to do things for God, but to be with Him. We should be people who accept His teachings, integrate ourselves with Him through His Word, His fellowship and His people, caring for others through His love.

External change, changing our actions, is good. But it's not enough. We need to change our orientation. We must be focused on God. Our roots must be fed by His Word and nourished by the Holy Spirit.

A tree, for example, takes years to develop deep roots and produce rich fruit. Christian maturity comes when our roots go deep into the soil of faith and our thoughts and imaginations are directed continually toward Him. Then our trunk grows larger and our limbs grow higher and we produce an abundance of fruit.

Obeying His teachings helps us grow to maturity in our faith and actions. Productive obedience results from His grace and law at work in our life.

Probably one of the greatest examples of actions producing thoughts is found in the way we treat our spouse. When we do kind acts for our spouse, before long, kind thoughts will be revived.

Discipline

Discipline may be the secret to success in the world. I've seen many people who have a solid foundation of intelligence and natural ability. Those who succeed are the ones who discipline themselves to build upon that foundation.

I've seen tremendous athletes succeed or fail because of their attitude toward their sport. If they're disciplined, they eat right and they train regularly. They're successful because they have a solid foundation. But those who rely solely on their physical abilities eventually fail.

In all walks of life, self-discipline makes the difference between people who succeed and those who fail.

But how does discipline apply to faith? Discipline takes what we know in our head and heart and applies it in our life. Discipline makes the difference between knowledge (what we know) and wisdom (how we live).

John Wesley had a tremendous amount of knowledge about God while he was at Oxford. But it was his faith that produced one of the greatest demonstrations of discipline the world has ever seen. His many books, his constant preaching, traveling and caring and ministering for others took an enormous amount of discipline. This all flowed from his transforming experience of faith at Aldersgate.

When we are tempted with thoughts that are inconsistent with Kingdom principles, we must discipline our mind to move on to godly thoughts. We must discipline our mind to focus on good thoughts of eternal significance. We can't dwell on those thoughts that are not full of faith. No one else can control our mind. We have to take responsibility for our thoughts and train ourselves on guiding and implementing those thoughts.

We must have spiritual discipline to follow God's commands. Yet our obedience isn't out of a sense of duty. Our obedience flows from the love we feel for Him and our desire to live in His promises.

> If you obey my commands, you will remain in my love, just as I have obeyed my Father's commands and remain in his love.
> **John 15:10**

We do what the Lord wants us to do because we love Him and have faith in His eternal promises. We find a greater satisfaction when our life is aligned with the Lord's will. Now, we may or may not be successful by worldly standards. But we reap a greater harvest. Our life glorifies God now and for eternity.

There will be times in our life when we lose sight of God's promises. We may be distracted by the promises of this world. We may begin to doubt God's word. Then our actions will reflect the imaginations that stem from those thoughts. And our world will come crashing down.

We will find no peace, and no productivity in life, when we live without faith in God's eternal sovereignty.

We must build a strong foundation by turning the Word of God into experience and relationship. The key is letting our obedience to Him provide the discipline we need.

> We want each of you to show this same diligence to the very end, in order to make your hope sure. We do not want you to become lazy, but to imitate those who through faith and patience inherit what has been promised.
> **Hebrews 6:11-12**

We need to build and rebuild on His promises. We need to return to our foundation—a sense of satisfaction in the life He has given us through Jesus Christ. May the actions of our life demonstrate the spiritual discipline that comes from living out the promises of God!

Setting Priorities

Is your mind filled with imaginations that are profitable and good—God's information? It's easy for us to allow our mind to be cluttered with imaginations that aren't really important and that prevent us from having abundant life in Christ.

Here's a quick exercise to measure your progress. Write down all the things you think about in a day—or an hour. Now, which are Christ-like and which are not?

One of the biggest dangers we have as Christians in controlling our mind is letting ourselves get too busy—filling our life with clutter. D.L. Moody polished the shoes of visitors when his students wouldn't. He showed that he wasn't too busy to act out his love for Christ by serving others.

Bill McCartney is the founder of Promise Keepers. He's also a former football coach. He would be the first person to tell us how vital it is to have a focused, controlled mind. It works not only on the football field, but in every arena of life. Being focused is what enables us to take on the mind of Christ.

Distractions can take us away from the mind of Christ. Our mind can get cluttered with thoughts that preoccupy us and detract from our relationship with the living, transforming God.

> But the worries of this life, the deceitfulness of wealth and the desires for other things come in and choke the word, making it unfruitful.
> **Mark 4:19**

Focusing on anything other than Christ will keep us from thinking like Him, worshipping Him, praying with Him and being with Him.

Each of us has interests we are passionate about, activities we love and enjoy. They can benefit us or they can harm us. It's a matter of our mindset and the priority we give these areas of our life. But when we worship these interests, when we order our life around them, they become idols. And we no longer are focused on Christ first.

As I mentioned earlier, I love to play the stock market. And with the economic boom in the past few years, the stock market was like a very lucrative poker game for me. A lot of people around me also were interested. We read reports, researched companies and followed business trends. We had computers galore as we watched the market's ups and downs. It was fun! But it also was distracting. It took time away from reading spiritual material and spending quiet time in my relationship with the Lord.

Now, there's nothing wrong with the stock market, and there's nothing wrong with the people who work hard with it. The market is wonderful in its proper place. But it can't take the place of our spiritual priorities. We can't let it distract us from taking on the mind of Christ.

Passionately, diligently, in every way possible, we should seek God.

You will seek me and find me when you seek
me with all your heart.
Jeremiah 29:13

We can't do everything in life. We have to set priorities, otherwise our mind and life become cluttered and unfocused. And the top priority is to focus on God, sharing our entire life with Him and always living in His presence.

Distractions take many forms. We frequently overload on life's demands and then find it difficult to make time to be with God. I've done that in my life. Haven't we all?

How do we know when something takes us from the mind of Christ? If it keeps us from growing in our relationship with Him. If it keeps us from worshipping Christ, from praying to Christ, from being with Christ. We need to put Christ back as our priority, and then give balance to these other interests.

We have to release the distractions so we can focus on God. Our thought processes, our behavior, our activities must reflect that focus.

There have been times in my life when I've had to eliminate other activities—which are pleasant and profitable—so I could choose pursuits that would allow me to think on Christ. Each of us has distractions that keep us from the essentials of Christ. We must avoid these so we can focus on the eternal view of Christ.

When we can rid ourselves of distractions, life becomes much simpler and more peaceful. We need to make life simple so we can become one with God. We need to do away with the other interests, the other gods, the other idols, that take our focus off God. We do not simplify our life for simplicity's sake. Rather, we simplify our life so we can focus more fully on God.

"Lord, teach us to be with You and to enjoy You in everything we do."

Meditate on God's Word

One of the people I know who was the closest to the Lord was my grandmother. She memorized the whole New Testament. She was with Christ because she had taken on the mind of Christ through her memory work. That memory work brought out a godly spirit. The Word of God within her made her radiate.

Think of it like this. When we're in love with someone, we read every one of their letters. We treasure them, we study them, we memorize them. Each word is precious because we're in love and the words reveal more about the person we love.

It's the same way with God. His letters to us are the Bible. When we're in love with Him, we study His Word, we read it with great passion. We hunger to hear more about Him and about how much He loves us.

Now, if we're not in love with another person, we may let their letters stack up in the mail on the kitchen counter. How often do we do that with God's Word?

Some people have said they've tried to read the Bible, but it hasn't worked out. Sometimes it's too difficult to read. Or they have trouble finding time to read. Or it doesn't seem to give them what they need.

Are these really excuses that we devise because we're not fully surrendered to Him? Sometimes we're still selfish and don't want to invest the time in reading His Word. Sometimes we're preoccupied with daily tasks and don't truly open our mind to what His Word can reveal.

To keep our mind focused on godly images, we must know God's Word. We need to constantly go over the Word to make our ways right.

How can a young man keep his way pure?
By living according to your word.
Psalm 119:9

Blessed is the man
who does not walk in the counsel of the wicked
or stand in the way of sinners
or sit in the seat of mockers.
But his delight is in the law of the Lord,
and on his law he meditates day and night.
Psalm 1:1-2

As we meditate on the Lord and His Word, our mind is filled with Him and we have fellowship with Him that brings victory and joy to our everyday living. We must think deliberately according to the Word of God. God will answer our questions through the Bible. We should study God's Word so we can apply it to our life and reason intelligently with it. Knowing the meaning of God's Word and growing in our ability to understand it will unlock spiritual meaning for us for our eternity.

God's grace and its power will change us. But we must let that grace lead us into following the Word of God, so we have a firm salvation and grow in the image of God. The Word is what makes us and cleanses us. Maturity comes from grace and the law, or God's Word, mingling in us. Then our imaginations of God become evident as we live according to His Word.

We can become so obsessed with the desires of the flesh and this world that we barely have enough time to acknowledge the Lord. We watch television, attend sporting events, find ourselves engrossed in our careers and our hobbies. We don't look at God's Word and find our real mind coming from that Word. We're not fulfilling our jobs as Christians.

We must read God's Word to make us His complete and adequate children, equipped for every good work and effective servants for Him.

> Do not let this Book of the Law depart from your mouth;
> meditate on it day and night, so that you may be careful
> to do everything written in it. Then you will be prosperous
> and successful. Have I not commanded you? Be strong
> and courageous. Do not be terrified; do not be discour-
> aged, for the Lord your God will be with you wherever
> you go.
> **Joshua 1:8-9**

We have to identify our heart and our mind with Christ so we will prosper because we are close to God. And we need to fix His Word firmly in our heart and mind so it can truly guide us.

> I have hidden your word in my heart
> that I might not sin against you.
> **Psalm 119:11**

One of the ways I keep God's Word in my heart is to memorize Scripture. Here are some of my favorites:

> Who shall separate us from the love of Christ? Shall
> trouble or hardship or persecution or famine or nakedness
> or danger or sword? As it is written:

> "For your sake we face death all day long;
> we are considered as sheep to be slaughtered."

> No, in all these things we are more than conquerors
> through him who loved us. For I am convinced that neither
> death nor life, neither angels nor demons, neither the
> present nor the future, nor any powers, neither height nor
> depth, nor anything else in all creation, will be able

to separate us from the love of God that is in
Christ Jesus our Lord.
Romans 8:35-39

Do not conform any longer to the pattern of this world,
but be transformed by the renewing of your mind. Then
you will be able to test and approve what God's will is—
his good, pleasing and perfect will.
Romans 12:2

If I speak in the tongues of men and of angels, but have not
love, I am only a resounding gong or a clanging cymbal.
If I have the gift of prophecy and can fathom all mysteries
and all knowledge, and if I have a faith that can move
mountains, but have not love, I am nothing. If I give all I
possess to the poor and surrender my body to the flames,
but have not love, I gain nothing. Love is patient, love is
kind. It does not envy, it does not boast, it is not proud.
It is not rude, it is not self-seeking, it is not easily angered,
it keeps no record of wrongs. Love does not delight in
evil but rejoices with the truth. It always protects, always
trusts, always hopes, always perseveres. Love never fails.
But where there are prophecies, they will cease; where
there are tongues, they will be stilled; where there is
knowledge, it will pass away. For we know in part and we
prophesy in part, but when perfection comes, the imperfect
disappears. When I was a child, I talked like a child, I
thought like a child, I reasoned like a child. When I became
a man, I put childish ways behind me. Now we see but a
poor reflection as in a mirror; then we shall see face to
face. Now I know in part, then I shall know fully, even as I
am fully known.

And now these three remain: faith, hope and love. But the
greatest of these is love.
I Corinthians 13

I have been crucified with Christ and I no longer live, but Christ lives in me. The life I live in the body, I live by faith in the Son of God, who loved me and gave himself for me.
Galatians 2:20

So that Christ may dwell in your hearts through faith. And I pray that you, being rooted and established in love, may have power, together with all the saints, to grasp how wide and long and high and deep is the love of Christ, and to know this love that surpasses knowledge—that you may be filled to the measure of all the fullness of God.
Ephesians 3:17-19

Be imitators of God, therefore, as dearly loved children.
Ephesians 5:1

Put on the full armor of God so that you can take your stand against the devil's schemes.
Ephesians 6:11

Rejoice in the Lord always. I will say it again: Rejoice! Let your gentleness be evident to all. The Lord is near. Do not be anxious about anything but in everything, by prayer and petition, with thanksgiving, present your requests to God. And the peace of God, which transcends all understanding, will guard your hearts and your minds in Christ Jesus.
Philippians 4:4-7

What we memorize is what we utilize. It's important that we memorize the Word of God and utilize its truths. Scripture that is merely read and not memorized is probably not utilized in our life. It's very important that we memorize Scripture so that we're in the habit of applying it daily in our life.

Using Bible Images

The Bible is full of images and symbols that we can use to guide our imaginations—God as our loving

Father, as our Shepherd, as our sovereign Lord, as our gracious King.

These images give us a fuller vision of God. They show us that we can always trust Him to provide for us, to love us, to forgive us, to heal us. Imaginations make faith an invigorating faith, a positive faith and joyful faith.

A very familiar chapter of the Bible is Psalm 23. It is full of images that God has designed to fill our thoughts: the shepherd, the sheep, the green pastures, the still waters, the dark valley, the shepherd's crook pulling us back on the path, the anointing of our head with oil.

All of these are pictures God has given us to fill our mind, to fill our imaginations and to fill our heart with faith. Here we see God's wisdom in the way the Bible is written, and how imaginations can help us live a life that honors God.

Our imaginations can captivate us with God. We want to embrace God. We know, in our head and in our heart, that His promises to us are real. These imaginations bring us a genuine sense of satisfaction and joy in the life God has given us. And our actions are guided by our satisfied imaginations.

Are our imaginations fixed on God, so that we have a mental picture of contentment? Or do we lose sight of God's promises and seek contentment in the goals and activities of this world—jobs, possessions, relationships, athletics and pastimes?

God's Word is an essential guide for our imaginations. We can use the examples of people in the Bible and apply the lessons they learned to our life. We can even picture ourselves in the Scriptures, envisioning ourselves as these people.

We can see ourselves as the leper coming to Jesus for healing. We can see ourselves as David, growing in faith and also struggling with deceit and death. We can see ourselves as Ruth, choosing the God of Israel as her all in all. Every person in the Bible is a part of us, and we can and should learn from their experiences.

These people show us, in positive and negative ways, how the foundation for godly living is godly thinking, and that godly thinking stems from imaginations that are satisfied with God.

Since, then, you have been raised with Christ, set your hearts on things above, where Christ is seated at the right hand of God. Set your minds on things above, not on earthly things.
Colossians 3:1-2

Paul tells us we need to focus on God first. We need to be satisfied with all He has given us. We don't need to search for fulfillment in the material goods and goals of this world. We will find ultimate satisfaction only in the loving arms of our Father.

Pray Without Ceasing

Do not be anxious about anything, but in everything, by prayer and petition, with thanksgiving, present your requests to God.
Philippians 4:6

A woman who worked at St. Luke's Cataract & Laser Institute, Jean Skinner, seemed to be in a continuous state of prayer. Jean's total relinquishment to Christ made her different from others, and that had a pronounced effect on everyone. She ministered constantly. She changed many lives in the community. She would lead four people to the Lord in one day. She affected the lives of the people in the churches she attended.

Jean would wake up at 5 a.m. and, with her prayer partner, would pray for 35 minutes to an hour. They would pray about everyone and the prayers would frequently be broken with laugher and joy.

Jean had a beautiful life, but it wasn't an easy one. In her early 30s, she was divorced, after an abusive marriage, with no formal education or training and no way to support herself. When she had nothing else to hold on to, she turned to the Lord. She overcame those obstacles by the strength of Jesus Christ. She grew close to a strong Pentecostal group, who believed every Word of the Lord and stood on it firmly—and who prayed firmly. Their total reliance on the Word and the person of Jesus Christ permeated her life. And even though she attended different churches for the next 20 years, she affected all the families she associated with. Her total reliance on God made her different from others.

By the world's standards, Jean didn't have anything. But as God sees it, she had everything. When she died at age 57 from cancer, all of us who knew her knew that she had gained what she could not lose. Her funeral was a joyous occasion because we all knew she was wrapped up in glory with the One she always thought about. The One she always sought to know. The One she loved with her whole heart and mind.

Jean's life holds a lesson for all of us. It seems to be a pattern that when we lose everything, we gain Christ. We don't have anything to hold onto besides Him. My father said, "You won't really hold onto Christ until that's the only thing you have to hold on to." It may be at one of the greatest points in our life—the greatest point of despair—when we seek Him.

We turn to Him in prayer. We unburden ourselves and surrender to Him. We talk, He listens. He talks, we listen. Prayer is an essential tool in conditioning our mind. How can we focus our thoughts on Him if we don't talk with Him and listen to his voice?

ACTS is the acronym to help us get started with a regular relationship of prayer: Adoration, Confession, Thanksgiving and Supplication.

ADORATION: We adore God, His sovereignty, His creation, His total control of the world, who He is. We fall in love with Him for His greatness. Adoration of the one we love and care for brings total joy.

> Sing to God, O kingdoms of the earth,
> sing praise to the Lord,
> to him who rides the ancient skies above,
> who thunders with mighty voice.
> Proclaim the power of God,
> whose majesty is over Israel,
> whose power is in the skies.

You are awesome, O God, in your sanctuary;
the God of Israel gives power and strength to his people.
Praise be to God!
Psalm 68:32-35

CONFESSION: God knows our sins. We know our sins. Confession is the vehicle for throwing away our sins, for casting off the burdens of our sin. We can tell the Lord about all the times we've failed Him in our thoughts and our actions. We certainly can't be arrogant or proud before Him because we have sinned against Him.

Yet we also show that we love Him because we clear the air of those sins; we pledge to start anew. And He gives us this fresh start.

If we confess our sins, he is faithful and just and will forgive us our sins and purify us from all unrighteousness.
I John 1:9

He wants us to have the positive attitude of loving Him, knowing that when we fail Him, we can confess our failings and He will still love us. This enables us to be free of guilt and not be depressed with the knowledge of wrongdoing.

THANKSGIVING: We are thankful to God for everything He is and will be, for everything He has done for us and everything He will do.

Thanksgiving changes us from cynical, critical, slothful people into energetic, enthusiastic, appreciative people. We are thankful we can come to Him in confession. We are thankful for His forgiveness.

Give thanks in all circumstances, for this is God's will for you in Christ Jesus.
I Thessalonians 5:18

SUPPLICATION: It's important that we "sup," that we're in supplication to God at all times. Do we ask God for everything or do we try to do it ourselves? We need to ask Him for our very substance. We need to live in His Jireh—His provision. We need to let Him take care of all our interpersonal relationships. We need to constantly practice His presence.

Call upon me in the day of trouble;
I will deliver you, and you will honor me.
Psalm 50:15

Adoration, confession, thanksgiving, supplication. All these elements are essential in any relationship. They are critical to the love, communication, forgiveness, respect, friendship and enjoyment found in relationships with others. They are truly important when we're talking about our Lord.

Our adoration of Him is simply respecting Him. Our confession means being honest with Him—just as we are honest in relationships with others. Thanksgiving to Him means the attitude of appreciation. Seeking supplication from Him shows that we trust Him to provide, knowing our needs are important to Him.

Tough Times

Do tough times and suffering affect our imaginations? Think of it this way: a tree is best measured when it is down. When we are felled by circumstances and events, we really find out what we're worth. Where do we turn for help? Do we selfishly want to control our own problems or do we surrender to God, in faith, knowing He will provide for us?

I know from personal experience that it is a gracious gift of God for us to suffer medically. I have struggled with broken legs. They take time to heal, and they don't always heal quickly and sometimes I've had to have further surgery. It's painful. It's frustrating. It tries my patience.

But this experience has revealed more to me about the gracious provision of God. I have been able to grow closer to Him because I've learned to endure and that has produced hope and love. It's frustrating when I'm self-centered. It's a joyous experience when I look to Christ first.

But he said to me, "My grace is sufficient for you, for my power is made perfect in weakness." Therefore I will boast all the more gladly about my weaknesses, so that Christ's power may rest on me. That is why, for Christ's sake, I delight in weaknesses, in insults, in hardships, in persecutions, in difficulties. For when I am weak, then I am strong.
II Corinthians 12:9-10

Much of our growth comes from our trials. Suffering weans us from selfishness and makes us see God's grace more clearly. When life is difficult, we have the opportunity to grow deeper with God in the experience of obedience. We learn more about His love, His grace, His provision.

It doesn't always happen that way. Especially in difficult times, we are susceptible to negative thoughts and imaginations. We can feel abandoned by God and become angry and bitter, worried and depressed. But we're not alone. He has promised He will always be with us!

Who shall separate us from the love of Christ? Shall trouble or hardship or persecution or famine or nakedness or danger or sword? As it is written:

"For your sake we face death all day long;
we are considered as sheep to be slaughtered."

No, in all these things we are more than conquerors through him who loved us. For I am convinced that neither death nor life, neither angels nor demons, neither the present nor the future, nor any powers, neither height nor depth, nor anything else in all creation, will be able to separate us from the love of God that is in Christ Jesus our Lord.
Romans 8:35-39

We will suffer in this life. We will find pain and grief and loss. Members of our families may disappoint us with their behavior. We may struggle in a relationship with family or friends. Our jobs won't always go well. But we will not suffer alone. We have the grace of God in our heart.

We must condition ourselves with this attitude in all tough times. C.K. Chesterton likened our trials to going through hot water.

- We must go through hot water. The good result is that we are cleaner.

- Genuine and fake diamonds look alike except under water. The genuine diamond still glows. The fake one is dull.

- The real joy in God is not diminished by troubles; it still sparkles.

We will be strengthened by tough times if we condition our mind to focus on God. If we are filled with His transforming faith, we will find rich blessings in adversity. But we must be vigilant in putting on the mind of Christ, rather than the worldly mind.

Let me share with you the experiences of Howard Rutledge. Rutledge was serving in Vietnam during the war when he was captured by the North Vietnamese. While he was a prisoner, he found the Lord in a very real way. This time of great trouble for him gave him a great relationship with the Lord.

I've seen God at work in my own struggles. About 30 years ago, when I first started my medical practice in the Tampa Bay area, I developed a large referral practice with optometrists. Things have changed since then, but in those days, it was unheard of for ophthalmologists to take referrals from optometrists. Other ophthalmologists got upset that I was working with optometrists and they thought I was getting a bigger share of the patient pie than I should have. Their jealousy shaped me. It made me determined to do an excellent job, always performing far above anything that could be criticized.

I moved to a different part of the area and established myself there. I knew that if I didn't move, the jealousies of my colleagues would hurt me. So I prayed for them and wished them well. I also used the situation to the glory of God and to the benefit of His kingdom. I dedicated my practice to God, and He has worked through me and those at St. Luke's to help thousands of patients through the years.

Imagine being in prison, charged falsely with a crime, not certain whether you'll live or die. That was Paul's situation as he sat in a Roman jail, a prisoner of the Emperor Nero. Was he worried? Full of discouragement and doubt? Feeling weary and depressed? Here's how he described his attitude in a letter to his friends in Philippi:

> I will continue to rejoice, for I know that through your
> prayers and the help given by the Spirit of Jesus Christ,
> what has happened to me will turn out for my deliverance.
> **Philippians 1:18-19**

Paul didn't say he would continue to endure his time in prison. Or that he would suffer but get through somehow. Or that he would struggle to get by or suffer silently. Instead, he rejoiced! He delighted in the presence of God!

> Rejoice in the Lord always. I will say it again: Rejoice!
> **Philippians 4:4**

Paul battled tough times with a thanksgiving frenzy! He worshiped His Savior!

Whatever trouble any child of God faces, we are never alone. We can always rely on our Creator with a spirit of thanksgiving.

> We do not want you to be uninformed, brothers,
> about the hardships we suffered in the province of Asia.
> We were under great pressure, far beyond our ability
> to endure, so that we despaired even of life. Indeed, in
> our hearts we felt the sentence of death. But this

happened that we might not rely on ourselves but on God, who raises the dead.
II Corinthians 1:8-9

When things seem more than we can endure, God shows us He will provide. We have His presence. And we can trust in God, who is so powerful He can raise the dead. Like Paul, we can find contentment in God, not in self and the world. This is Jesus' promise to us:

> I have told you these things, so that in me you may have peace. In this world you will have trouble. But take heart! I have overcome the world.
> **John 16:33**

Know that whatever we face, Christ has faced it first. And He has conquered it for us! The God of all grace gives us His grace for each circumstance and trial—for financial trials, for family trials, for relationship trials, for medical trials. In all areas, God's grace is sufficient. May each of us see beyond sufferings and trials to eternal glory. Paul explains it this way:

> I consider that our present sufferings are not worth comparing with the glory that will be revealed in us.
> **Romans 8:18**

We may be tempted to focus on our current suffering, pain and disappointment. But we can counter those negative imaginations with a focus on the glory that will be revealed in eternity. But not just in eternity. We also have the Spirit's help, giving us hope and faith in the present times of suffering, which is really the glory of God already in us. The glory has already begun. The glory is manifest in us now! And we eagerly await its fullness in the future.

How do we get such glory? Through the Lord Jesus Christ. Jesus says:

> I have given them the glory that you gave me, that they may be one as we are one: I in them and you in me.
> **John 17:22-23**

Now, we may not see this glory. Indeed, it's not visible to us in our current earthly condition. And it's certainly not visible to the world. Without looking through imaginations of Jesus, no one can see this glory. But through the process of maturing in our faith, it becomes more visible.

In the midst of trials, non-believers may ask why we seem at peace, why we have a positive attitude. They may wonder about the "pill" we're on. The pill is faith. Our needs have been supplied. We have nothing to prove to the world. We know who is in control, we know who is sovereign, we know who is our daily, and eternal, rest.

We need to think of our times of trouble and sorrow as times that prepare us, with great anticipation, to being engulfed in God's presence forever. That imagination will encourage us, motivate us, strengthen us and support us.

We let our imaginations be focused on God in the present and in eternity, putting everything else in the background. Knowing God as He is known in eternity provides us with peace during troubled times. Our faith in His promises, finding satisfaction in Him, leads to overflowing peace.

Fighting Doubt

Imagine you are being confronted by a hostile crowd about whether you are a follower of Christ. You're worried they could arrest or even kill you. Would your faith sustain you in such a moment?

There are times when all of us doubt God's promises. If Peter, the foremost of the apostles, had doubts, why should we be any different?

When we begin to doubt, we need to go back to His Word and re-read His promises. We need to spend time talking with God in prayer. We need to search out reinforcement with our Christian friends. We need to review our life and remember the mighty things God has done for us. We need to remember the power of the one in whom we trust!

Some trust in chariots and some in horses,
but we trust in the name of the Lord our God.
Psalm 20:7

Our faith is re-awakened when we realize His promises are true for each of us. Then our mind finds its full satisfaction in Him. Our thoughts and actions are focused on Him. We glorify Him by being satisfied in Him.

> Though you have not seen him, you love him; and even though you do not see him now, you believe in him and are filled with an inexpressible and glorious joy, for you are receiving the goal of your faith, the salvation of your souls.
> **I Peter 1:8-9**

What a glorious promise! We believe without seeing, and that belief leads to our eternal life and salvation of our souls.

We all wrestle with our questions and doubts about God. "Who is our Creator? Does He live? Does He love? Does He forgive? Does He provide forever? How does He do it?"

The Old Testament tells us how Jacob wrestled.

> So Jacob was left alone, and a man wrestled with him till daybreak. When the man saw that he could not overpower him, he touched the socket of Jacob's hip so that his hip was wrenched as he wrestled with the man.
> **Genesis 32:24-25**

Still the man could not defeat Jacob. And Jacob would not let him go until he revealed himself. Finally the man blessed Jacob, and Jacob, who was renamed Israel, knew what he had encountered.

> I saw God face to face, and yet my life was spared.
> **Genesis 32:30**

This is the wrestling we all encounter. Now few of us become Israel. Few of us have an intimate physical encounter. But we still struggle.

The result of wrestling for Jacob was a broken hip. He spent the rest of his life with a limp. Sometimes we're broken in some way as a result of our struggles. But when we're broken of our pride, our selfishness, our other sins, we can more fully submit our mind to Him. We become more effective children of God.

We need to hold fast to our imagination of a life of faith. We have to make faith the foundation upon which we build our imaginations.

We cannot let the imaginations of this world detract from our focus on God. It's difficult to overcome the thoughts of this world—worries, coveting money, possessions, relationships, success.

But remember, if our thoughts are not rooted in faith, they are sinful. They will destroy us. Instead, let us focus on the power and strength of the Almighty Lord. He overshadows any events and circumstances in this life on earth. He gives us new strength!

> Do you not know?
> Have you not heard?
> The Lord is the everlasting God,
> the Creator of the ends of the earth.
> He will not grow tired or weary,
> and his understanding no one can fathom.
> He gives strength to the weary
> and increases the power of the weak.
> Even youths grow tired and weary,
> and young men stumble and fall;
> but those who hope in the Lord
> will renew their strength.
> They will soar on wings like eagles,
> they will run and not grow weary,
> they will walk and not be faint.
> **Isaiah 40:28-31**

We can feel overwhelmed by the struggles and battles in this world. But God understands. He created us. He knows us intimately. He walks with us every day. Turning to Him in faith will renew our strength and our energy. We are not alone! We have the power of the living God.

Getting Rid of Bad Thoughts

When we attempt to control our thoughts we have two approaches, a negative one and a positive one. The negative approach is to say, "Oh, the heck with those thoughts," and try to drive them out ourselves. Sometimes I've even pictured myself vomiting to rid myself of worldly thoughts. But this approach has a negative effect on our whole personality and on the way we think. We think we can do it ourselves, and we become critical and full of criticism. Negative ideas produce negative results.

The best way is to turn the thoughts over to Jesus. We can say, "Jesus, take over this thought. Thank you for what you've given to me. I appreciate you taking care of this problem. Give me greater endurance and greater character so I can have greater hope."

We need to cast out the parts of our life that produce worldly thoughts. We need to say goodbye to them and not return to them.

> As a dog returns to its vomit,
> so a fool repeats his folly.
> **Proverbs 26:11**

This verse says we're foolish if we allow our mind to return to vain imaginations. Do we allow our mind to return to the "vomit"? Do we stay sick? Do we remain foolish if we open up again the ungodly parts of our mind? We can only cast out these thoughts with the help of Christ.

Once we are aware of wrong thoughts, we must quickly return our focus to God and cleanse our mind through His power.

Choosing the Right Companions

I had an employee whom I hired shortly after her 20th birthday. She was bright, beautiful, witty and a minister's daughter. She seemed to have everything going for her. Growing up in a Christian home, she accepted Christ as her personal Savior at an early age.

After moving to Florida with her family, she couldn't find the right peer group. While she still professed Christ as her

Savior, she was no longer satisfied in Him. She became impatient for a romantic relationship in this new location where she didn't have her lifelong friends. It wasn't long before she became infatuated with a considerably older man. She began lying to her parents and seeing the man against their wishes. He was good looking and very persuasive. He challenged the very core of her beliefs and soon filled her mind with ungodly imaginations. She never anticipated that his influence could be so strong. He wooed her and convinced her of his supposedly undying love. It wasn't too long before he had her thinking worldly thoughts.

Most of us know someone with a similar experience and the all-too-common ending to the familiar story. This bright, beautiful, witty daughter of a minister became pregnant. In mere months, her ungodly friend had influenced her imaginations and practically erased her lifetime of Christian upbringing.

She was unable to resist temptation because her imaginations were no longer focused on Christ. If she had been satisfied in Christ, she would have been able to trust God with her desire for a romantic relationship. She would not have been deluded by false imaginations that caused her to be attracted to a sinful man and then to commit sin.

Because of God's amazing grace, this story has a happy ending. II Chronicles 16:9 says, "For the eyes of the Lord range throughout the earth to strengthen those whose hearts are fully committed to him." As her family interceded in prayer and trusted God for His provision in their daughter's life, God's Spirit faithfully, gently brought back imaginations of Christ and His redeeming love to her.

All the Scriptures and biblical principles she had learned throughout her childhood once again filled her mind. Her decision became clear: She would not marry this manipulative man; instead she would be a single mom and raise her child to know God. She confessed her sin, severed the relationship and once again focused on Christ and His ability to provide for all her needs. Her imaginations were filled with dependence on the God who loved her so much that He forgave her.

Her immediate family, her church family and her St. Luke's family stood with her and supported her decision. She gave birth to a wonderful, healthy baby boy, lived with her parents and continued working at St. Luke's, all the while filling her mind with God's faithful promises that He would take care of her and her baby. And He did. Today, she is married, has another child and is faithfully living for Jesus, totally committed to His purposes for her life. She chooses her friends very carefully and fills her family's life with people who love God.

It's important that we direct our thoughts toward God and keep them focused on Him. Yet it's equally important how we choose the people we are with. People affect our thoughts. We should surround ourselves with people who are focused on God and want to grow in the Lord as much as we do. We have to be selective and sometimes say no to people—even if they seem exciting and interesting. True excitement and friendship come through sharing our life in Jesus Christ. We can't always choose all our friends. But we can focus on sharing our life—and our struggles—with those who are also seeking a closer relationship with God.

> My son, pay attention to what I say;
> listen closely to my words.
> Do not let them out of your sight,
> keep them within your heart;
> for they are life to those who find them
> and health to a man's whole body.
> Above all else, guard your heart,
> for it is the wellspring of life.
> **Proverbs 4:20-23**

Avoiding the Wrong Situations

In addition to taking hold of our thoughts, we need to change the actions that produce those thoughts. If there are places that produce vain imaginations, we must avoid those places. If there are activities and events that keep us from maturing in Christ, we must choose not to participate. Anything that keeps us from taking on the mind of Christ should be eliminated from our life. We must avoid putting ourselves in situations that compromise our moral convictions. While we must be in the world, we don't have to let the world be in us.

A Cure for the Worry Disease

ARE YOU WORRIED RIGHT NOW? ARE YOU AFRAID? MANY OF US HAVE FACED FEARS ABOUT ECONOMIC PROBLEMS OR LOSSES, PHYSICAL DISTRESS, PHYSICAL SAFETY OR VIOLENCE. SOME PEOPLE ARE WORRIED OR AFRAID ALL THE TIME. ANXIETY IS THE WORD OF THIS AGE. AND WORRY IS ONE OF THE TOUGHEST BATTLES WE FACE IN CONDITIONING OUR MINDS.

As an ophthalmologist, I see patients every day. It's easy to tell the ones who are chronically worried. They are critical about the people and places around them. They are judgmental. They have trouble making decisions because worry preoccupies their minds. And worry affects their health. It makes them tired. It suppresses their immune system, leaving them more susceptible to sickness and disease. Worry can destroy their entire body.

There's good news! God hears our cries. He will take care of us. If we have truly surrendered to Him, and are resting in Him as Paul did in Galatians 2:20, there is no room for worry.

Put yourself in the place of an Old Testament man named Jabez. His mother had named him Jabez, which sounds like the Hebrew word for pain, saying, "I gave birth to him in pain" (I Chronicles 4:9). The Bible tells us that he was more honorable than his brothers. And he called on God.

Jabez cried out to the God of Israel, "Oh, that you would bless me and enlarge my territory! Let your hand be with

me, and keep me from harm so that I will be free from pain." And God granted his request.
I Chronicles 4:10

God heard this man's request. He blessed Jabez, giving him pardon, peace, purpose, power. God kept His hand on Jabez, protecting him and guiding him.

From Genesis to Revelation, God promises to keep us in His hands. Those hands save us, heal us, carry us, care for us, support us, love us, redeem us and sustain us. They are always with us. They will keep us for eternity. No matter how worn down and discouraged, how worried and anxious, we are still in His hands.

All of us worry. The rich worry that they're going to lose everything, and the poor worry that they aren't going to have enough. It's hard to know who worries the most. But we do know who worries the least—the people who know their ultimate reality is future grace with Jesus Christ.

Come to me, all you who are weary and burdened, and I will give you rest. Take my yoke upon you and learn from me, for I am gentle and humble in heart, and you will find rest for your souls. For my yoke is easy and my burden is light.
Matthew 11:28-30

Faith is the reasoned response to revealed truth. When we believe God's promises are true for us, fear leaves. Worry leaves. Anxiety leaves.

When our life is centered on satisfaction in Him, we have peace that comes from knowing the all-sovereign God and understanding His almighty grace.

Peace I leave with you; my peace I give you. I do not give to you as the world gives. Do not let your hearts be troubled and do not be afraid.
John 14:27

True peace is based on the sovereignty of God. We aren't going to be able to explain God because we aren't God. He is beyond our comprehension. We simply live by faith in our God.

The peace of God silences the troubles in our spirit. The Gospel gives us a quiet heart. We get a clearer image of God as Jehovah-Shalom—the Lord is Peace. We are filled with the peace of God, which comes from worshipping God, trusting God, having God within us and being in His kingdom of faith.

We need to integrate the concept of God's sovereignty into our lives. Then His grace is manifest, His future grace becomes our contemplation, and we find our right place with Him. He truly becomes our Father, our Provider, the Eternal One.

When we know God as Jehovah-Jireh, as our Father and as our Shepherd, grace and peace are multiplied. Worry and other mindsets of selfishness can no longer dominate our life. He is the King and the Lord of our life.

All things exist because of the power of God. We should stand in amazement and wonder at the power of the sovereign God. We have nothing to fear. Nevertheless, we tend to forget, at times, how powerful God is. He raised up Jesus! He has the power to do anything—even destroy death.

God who gives life to the dead and calls things that are not as though they were.
Romans 4:17

Actually, death could not hold God, in the person of Jesus, because He is by nature so powerful that it was impossible for death to hold Him. The great power in Jesus enabled Him to rise. That great power enables us to rise with Him. His power of resurrection becomes our power of eternal life.

There's a story about a couple who had been married many years. One day, the husband drowned. His wife's comment was, "My God is in the heavens." She knew God's sovereignty. She knew He would care for her. She knew her husband was fellowshipping with God in heaven. Certainly she grieved over the loss of her husband. But she found comfort in the presence of the sovereign God.

Dr. Beb Morris says the more secure we are, the less we react to fear. When we are secure in Christ, we're not afraid. We must focus our mind on Christ, and He will help us feel secure, even in situations that could make us worry.

> For God did not give us a spirit of timidity,
> but a spirit of power, of love and of self-discipline.
> **II Timothy 1:7**

We stand on Calvary! We stand on the resurrection of our Lord, Jesus Christ! Our confidence in Christ overcomes any insecurity, any worry, any fear. We're totally new beings with Him because we know we'll be with Him forever.

All of us should have such certainty in our faith. Yet there are times, even when we know God's presence is with us, that we face fear and doubt. Even the disciples, who lived in the physical presence of Christ, were afraid.

> Then he got into the boat and his disciples followed him. Without warning, a furious storm came up on the lake, so that the waves swept over the boat. But Jesus was sleeping. The disciples went and woke him, saying, "Lord, save us! We're going to drown!"
>
> He replied, "You of little faith, why are you so afraid?" Then he got up and rebuked the winds and the waves, and it was completely calm.
>
> The men were amazed and asked, "What kind of man is this? Even the winds and the waves obey him!"
> **Matthew 8:23-27**

The disciples had lost sight of Jesus' sovereignty. They were frightened by the storm. Jesus had to remind them, once again, to have faith in Him. He demonstrated His mighty power. He showed them how He was in control. And the disciples marveled at this man who calmed the water. If He can do that, how much more can He do?

In our life, we will face storms of trouble. Now imagine Jesus with us in those storms, in the same boat. He will calm the seas. He will calm our heart. He has a commanding power over the wind and the water. He has a commanding power over all the elements that affect our life and toss us around every day. We should not focus on the storms. Instead, may we focus on the power that keeps us safe.

Now, we all have been hurt by bad choices, bad experiences, bad relationships, even addictions. The results of those actions can destroy our confidence; they can damage our ability to trust in God. We can become insecure, angry and fearful.

But remember, Christ loves us, even when we believe we're not worthy of that love. His grace is sufficient for all the thoughts and experiences in our life. He will deliver us from desperate situations. He will meet all of our needs. He will restore us and renew our confidence when we place our trust in Him.

This is a lesson the disciples struggled to learn. Jesus sent the disciples ahead of Him in a boat. After His time of prayer, He walked across the lake to them. The disciples were scared; they thought it was a ghost walking across the water. Jesus had to calm them down and tell them it was Him. But Peter put Jesus to the test.

> "Lord, if it's you," Peter replied, "tell me to come to you on the water."
> "Come," he said.
> Then Peter got down out of the boat, walked on the water and came toward Jesus. But when he saw the wind, he was afraid and, beginning to sink, cried out, "Lord, save me!"
> Immediately Jesus reached out his hand and caught him. "You of little faith," he said, "why did you doubt?"
>
> And when they climbed into the boat, the wind died down. Then those who were in the boat worshiped him, saying,

"Truly you are the Son of God."
Matthew 14:28-33

Peter could walk on the water as long as he trusted Jesus. But the wind shook his faith and he began to sink into the water. Once again, we see Jesus reaching out His mighty hand to save Peter.

Jesus will reach out to each of us, too. When the wind and the waves batter us, when we feel we're drowning and we begin to worry and feel afraid, we need to remember that He is there. His loving arms will keep us safe. He is our confidence!

Trusting in those powerful arms is an important factor that prevents worry. We need to believe in God's sovereignty and in His power to care for us. The Bible tells us numerous times not to worry. We must trust in the Lord with all our heart. He is the Almighty God. His power is limitless and His love for us is beyond measure!

"Have faith in God," Jesus answered. "I tell you the truth, if anyone says to this mountain, 'Go, throw yourself into the sea,' and does not doubt in his heart but believes that what he says will happen, it will be done for him."
Mark 11:22-23

What a powerful promise! God can, and will, do anything when we ask in total faith. That degree of faith and trust will destroy any worry that creeps into our imaginations.

Yet some people find it difficult to trust. They say, or at least think, "If you trust anybody, you're a fool." They tend to be skeptical, cynical and adversarial in all sorts of situations. These folks are living in a prison of their own making. Richard Lovelace wrote, in his poem *To Althea from Prison* in 1649, "Stone walls do not a prison make."

Fear, doubt, worry. These are the building blocks that will imprison us. We can become slaves to our emotions. It affects our relationship with others. Most important, it affects our relationship with God.

If we have trouble trusting people, whom we see and with whom we come into physical contact, we have even greater trouble trusting God, whom we find invisible. Those truly imprisoned by fear and worry see no evidence of God in their life. They might go through the motions of asking Him for help, but they doubt that He will actually provide.

He who doubts is like a wave of the sea, blown and tossed by the wind. That man should not think he will receive anything from the Lord; he is a double-minded man, unstable in all he does.
James 1:6-8

Doubt destroys the satisfaction we find in God's promises. We lose our image of God as Creator and Provider. We no longer have a mindset of trust. Our foundation of faith is shaky.

We will worry until we focus on the person of Jesus Christ. Remember, the Lord Jireh will provide for all those who put their faith in Him. When we find satisfaction in His provision, when we turn our minds to imagining His promises, when we worship Him as the disciples did, we will be freed from worry. We are filled with His peace.

When I begin to worry, I picture myself being in God's heaven, running through the clouds with some of the people who were great runners. Of course, I'll be far behind them. Their style and technique are far greater than mine. But I imagine running through those golden streets of heaven in a state of maximum love with my Lord.

Those imaginations allow me to focus on His future grace, a grace that will allow me to be with Him and experience His care for eternity.

Our eternal life in that kingdom is the greatest assurance of peace. We worry less about the circumstances and events of this world because we know a greater world. We are transformed because we have confidence in Christ. This imagination demolishes worry!

Numbered with the Transgressors

WE CAN LOOK TO JESUS AS OUR ROLE MODEL OF A SATISFIED MIND. BUT BECAUSE HE WAS DIVINE, WAS IT EASIER FOR HIM TO BE ABANDONED TO GOD?

The prophet Isaiah reminds us that Jesus also was human and that He had very human struggles.

> He had no beauty or majesty to attract us to him,
> nothing in his appearance that we should desire him.
> He was despised and rejected by men,
> a man of sorrows, and familiar with suffering.
> Like one from whom men hide their faces
> he was despised, and we esteemed him not.
> **Isaiah 53:2-3**

Jesus never got the easy way out during His life on earth. He wasn't particularly handsome, which would have helped Him get some attention. More than that, He didn't have a very pleasant life. He didn't have a home, a regular place to sleep. He had to live on the generosity of others. And many had a very low opinion of Him—they weren't very generous.

> While Jesus was having dinner at Matthew's house, many tax collectors and "sinners" came and ate with Him and His disciples. When the Pharisees saw this, they asked His disciples, "Why does your teacher eat with tax collectors and 'sinners'?"
>
> On hearing this, Jesus said, "It is not the healthy who need a doctor, but the sick. But go and learn what this means: 'I

desire mercy, not sacrifice.' For I have not come to call the righteous, but sinners."
Matthew 9:10-13

Jesus is our doctor. He understands our sinful condition. He knows how to heal our wounds and give peace to our souls. But not solely from a clinical, objective view. Isaiah describes Jesus' own suffering, and how that intimately binds us to Him.

Therefore I will give him a portion among the great,
and he will divide the spoils with the strong,
because he poured out his life unto death,
and was numbered with the transgressors.
For he bore the sin of many,
and made intercession for the transgressors.
Isaiah 53:12

Christ was numbered with us; He was considered one of us. Christ was bruised and beaten for us. He was crucified for us. He was bound together with you and with me.

My heart overflows from that image of a suffering Christ. He took on my sins and paid for them with His own blood. He healed me. He restored me to relationship with God the Father. He redeemed me with His precious blood. There is no greater satisfaction. He loves me so much that He paid a great price for me. And I live in His provision now and for eternity.

When each of us finds our full measure of satisfaction in the grace of our glorious Lord, we must then bind ourselves with our fellow sinners. In living out our image of Christ, we need to be bound with all other people who sin—and that's everybody. Fellow believers in Christ sin. Non-believers sin. All of us are sinners. Nobody is an exception. It is only through Christ's grace that we are saved. We cannot earn it. And we can't expect others to earn their salvation.

So we must consider ourselves, in our mind of Christ, to be "numbered with the transgressors." We need to be understanding. We need to be intercessors rather than accusers. We need to suffer with others and feel their burdens as Christ suffered for us.

A young man I know is one of the best examples of leading a life that is "numbered with the transgressors." He manages an office building for me. His wife's family has been involved in the Christian musical world for many years. They have three wonderful boys.

This young man extends himself to people who have been in all kinds of trouble—drug and alcohol abusers, thieves and con artists. He does more than wish them well. He brings them into his home, he ministers to them, he suffers with them. Sometimes, he even suffers because of them. Yes, these folks occasionally have stolen from him. Once, someone took something he valued greatly and sold it to get money to buy drugs. Yet I've seen this man accept these "transgressors" back into his house and family. He keeps on loving them and persevering because he never thinks of himself as better than they are. He considers himself an equal transgressor.

I have tried to help some doctors who were kicked out of the medical society. I thought they were good doctors who just had a poor understanding of people. And I ended up being hurt by them.

It doesn't always work out well when we try to help others. We may try to help people, only to have them take our money and never return it. Or we've tried to help those who have substance abuse problems, only to have them leave us hurt, confused and disappointed. The cost to be numbered with the transgressors is high.

Six or seven years ago, a doctor who worked with me left his wife and kids. He married a second time, then divorced that wife and married for a third time. He and his third wife had a child. While all this was happening, I was somewhat arrogant. I emotionally distanced myself from the situation and tried not to care about whether he was destroying himself. Then I realized that I, too, could have been in a similar situation. In a new way, I realized how I was numbered with the transgressors.

Being numbered with the transgressors is more than intellectually trying to help someone. It's realizing that we could be, and possibly are, in the same situation. We can and do fail. We are all sinners in God's eyes.

Another friend of mine recently left his family. Then he got involved in another relationship that was going to end badly. Instead of being arrogant and withdrawn, I numbered myself with him.

I contacted one of his closest friends, and the three of us started spending time together. We let him know we were with him and felt his suffering, confusion and pain. And we prayed for him. This man ended up going back to his wife, and he has a much stronger relationship now. The lesson for me is to be humble and loving.

Paul, the great apostle, missionary, preacher and writer, probably had more reason than most to feel slightly arrogant from his position of authority in the church. But he didn't. One example shows how he considered himself among the most humble by identifying with a runaway slave, Onesimus, who had robbed his master and escaped to Rome. In Rome, through Paul's ministry he became a follower of Christ.

Paul knew Onesimus had run away and that it was time for him to go back. He also knew Onesimus had a debt that needed to be paid back to his owner, Philemon. Philemon was a fairly prominent man in the city of Colossae. He was also a follower of Christ, and Paul considered him a good friend. So Paul sent Onesimus back, with a letter in hand from Paul to Philemon.

> If he has done you any wrong or owes you anything, charge it to me...I will pay it back.
> **Philemon 1:18, 19**

Paul asked Philemon to spare Onesimus and let him take over the debts. He also speaks to Philemon as a friend.

> So if you consider me a partner, welcome him [Onesimus] as you would welcome me.
> **Philemon 1:17**

Paul considered himself equal with Onesimus. But that's not to say he considered Onesimus as good as he is. Instead, he considered himself an equal sinner to Onesimus.

He lived out the attitude of Christ that he described in his letter to the church at Philippi.

> Who, being in very nature God,
> did not consider equality with God something to be grasped,
> but made himself nothing,
> taking the very nature of a servant,
> being made in human likeness.
> **Philippians 2:6-7**

Paul tells us that we should have the same attitude. We are to serve others, knowing that we are not better than they are, but that we are all equal. Christ makes us equal. All who are saved are saved by His matchless, boundless grace alone!

CHAPTER 2 1

Letting Our Light Shine

IF WE ARE TRULY SATISFIED WITH GOD'S PROMISES, CAN WE STILL HAVE A NEGATIVE ATTITUDE? IS OUR ATTITUDE AFFECTED BY OUR LEVEL OF SATISFACTION? HOW DOES OUR DAILY LIFE FLOW IF WE'RE FEELING POSITIVE? HOW ABOUT WHEN WE'RE FEELING NEGATIVE?

The Bible tells us what our attitude should be when we are focused on walking with God every day:

> Blessed are those who have learned to acclaim you,
> who walk in the light of your presence, O Lord.
> They rejoice in your name all day long;
> they exult in your righteousness.
> **Psalm 89:15-16**

These verses tell us that we should be filled with joy when we are truly satisfied with God's promises. We walk in the light of God's presence. Therefore, we no longer are negative and critical people. It's the difference between being a "light" or a "shadow".

"Light" has many meanings. First and foremost, Christ uses this word to describe Himself.

> I am the light of the world. Whoever follows me will never walk in darkness, but will have the light of life.
> **John 8:12**

Light also means illuminating and brightening everything around us, being informed and so on. On the other hand, shadows take away. They make objects difficult to see and understand. Jesus tells us we should be lights if we are His followers.

You are the light of the world.
Matthew 5:14

Our light is the light of Christ shining through us. We're like the moon, reflecting the light of the sun. On our own, we give little light. But when we align with the Son, we can be very powerful. We shine with God's truth, reflecting His love.

Paul tells us how to be lights in this dark, confusing world:

Do everything without complaining or arguing, so that you may become blameless and pure, children of God without fault in a crooked and depraved generation, in which you shine like stars in the universe.
Philippians 2:14-15

Let me give you an example. At a recent conference I attended, many of the physicians were complaining about how insurance reimbursements for cataract surgery had been cut 60 percent in the past 10 years. I certainly sympathized with their complaints. Many of us have done more work and made less money during the last 10 years. The complaints increased as more doctors expressed their feelings. The unhappiness fed on itself. As I listened to the growing number of complaints, I realized just how important is the attitude I have, and the attitude my colleagues have.

I looked around at the doctors who were complaining. They didn't look as though they had physically suffered because their reimbursement income had dropped. When it was my turn to talk, I reminded them that we should be thankful now more than ever. After all, through medical advances we can now help people in a greater way. But these doctors wanted to feel bad because they thought they had been mistreated.

What about us? Are we lights who offer praise, encouragement and appreciation? Or are we shadows, who are negative, critical and selfish? Do we love our work and display a positive attitude, or do we resent our work, displaying a lack of motivation and a poor attitude?

What about relationships with others? Do we contribute positively or negatively in relationships? Do we appreciate our children and their status in life? Do we encourage them or criticize them? Do we enjoy their presence? Do we treat our spouse as a partner or a marital servant—to be ordered about, rather than loved and appreciated?

Clebe McClary is an excellent example of a Christ-centered attitude. He's an accomplished marathon runner who can stay on a treadmill longer than just about anyone in his age group.

His feats are even more remarkable because he lost an arm and an eye. His book, *Living Proof*, talks about his attitude. "In this world of give and take, there are not enough people who are willing to give what it takes," he says.

A God-centered attitude is based on our abilities. For example, we can have an attitude that we're going to get in a boxing ring and face Muhammad Ali in his prime, but we're going to take a licking. Our abilities must be developed to go along with our attitude. Our faith is rooted in the blessings we receive as the children of God. We focus on the positive imaginations of Christ. It's more than thinking random good thoughts and hoping vaguely for the best. We are taking on the mind of Christ.

The foundation for a positive attitude is our unshakable faith in God's provision.

And we know that in all things God works for
the good of those who love him, who have been
called according to his purpose.
Romans 8:28

One of the great ophthalmologists in our era is a light—Dr. Jim Rowsey. He is a man who truly loves God and lives according to His purpose.

Dr. Rowsey is the physician who treated the very first patient in the United States with the VISX-Taunton Excimer Laser once FDA approval had been granted. He is the VISX principal certifying surgeon in the state of Florida, and has trained more eye surgeons to perform refractive surgery than any other clinician in the state. Dr. Rowsey designed the first computerized corneal topography device for measuring refractive surgery results.

He loves his work as an ophthalmologist. His enthusiasm and excitement are contagious, electrifying all the people around him. He is an effective presence in his world. In meetings, he consistently offers a positive way to solve problems. A difficult diagnosis is always a challenge, not a defeat. He considers alternate management of medical problems. In surgery, he always looks for a better way to care for patients.

Dr. Rowsey's enthusiasm and joyous attitude are displayed in all areas of his life. He says joy comes to us as we share it. He firmly believes that a spirit of joy in our life shines out and affects everyone around us. He says, "When I have 10 phone calls to return at the end of the day, I have made a decision to smile at the telephone before I dial the phone—it's never smiled back at me—and to continue smiling as the phone is ringing. Then my joy at hearing the patient's voice is recognized by the patient as they answer the phone."

He tells a beautiful illustration of exactly how this decision of joy works and affects others. He accompanied his 3-year-old granddaughter to the ice-skating rink for one of her first lessons. As they together crept around the edge of the ice rink, holding onto the railing, she fell down every foot or so. Each time, she valiantly pulled herself back up, grabbing the rail with both hands.

She was undaunted by the trauma of continuous defeat and began singing throughout the ordeal, "I have the JOY, JOY, JOY, JOY down in my heart. Where? Down in my heart. Where? Down in my heart..." She sang over and over again with each fall.

As they labored around the rink, an elderly man standing by the side was scowling at the display of skaters. He just wasn't enjoying himself one bit, and right in front of him, she took another fall. For the umpteenth time, she pulled herself up and sang right into the scowling man's face. "I have the JOY, JOY, JOY, JOY down in my heart…"

Instantly the scowling man's frown became a smile! He couldn't help it, as he recognized the decision to keep singing in the face of falling. He caught contagious joy from a little one determined to have a smile and song regardless of the circumstance.

Each of us can be light and joy to others, showing a Christ-like attitude from imaginations that are filled with His Word:

> By joyful always; pray continually; give thanks in all circumstances, for this is God's will for you in Christ Jesus.
> **I Thessalonians 5:16-18**

Our challenge every day is to align our imaginations with Christ. Our pure and complete satisfaction comes from believing His promises and following His commandments—acting out His commandments in our life. Our mind cannot only contain the thoughts; it must contain the attitude of carrying through those promises.

> Do not conform any longer to the pattern of this world, but be transformed by the renewing of your mind. Then you will be able to test and approve what God's will is—his good, pleasing and perfect will.
> **Romans 12:2**

God is most glorified when we are satisfied in Him. Every day, let us seek His mind, His heart, His joy and His peace. Every day, let us seek His pure and perfect will. Every day, let us rejoice in the eternal promises He has made us. Every day, let us find our *shalom* in our relationship with Him.

Abandoned to God

I'M NOT MUCH OF A GOLFER, BUT I'VE PLAYED A FEW ROUNDS THROUGH THE YEARS. AND THERE'S ONE THING I'VE LEARNED FROM PLAYING GOLF. IF I IMAGINE THAT I CAN PLAY WELL AND I'M SATISFIED WITH MY PERFORMANCE, I USUALLY HAVE A GOOD GAME. BUT IF I'M FRUSTRATED WITH THE GAME AND HAVE IMAGES OF A PUTT GOING AWRY, IT USUALLY DOES. OF COURSE, MY SKILL LEVEL DETERMINES TO SOME EXTENT THE WAY I PLAY. BUT MORE IMPORTANTLY, I'VE LEARNED THAT THE GAME IS IN MY HEAD.

My imaginations affect how well I perform. I can choose to try and play the perfect game, but never be happy out on the course. I can be negative, criticizing and second-guessing every move. Or I can find satisfaction in just being out there, doing my best and enjoying my efforts.

This lesson doesn't apply solely to golf. A sense of satisfaction in my daily life, rooted in godly imaginations, is essential if I am going to find a peaceful and joyous life filled with meaningful relationships and actions.

As we mature in our faith and develop our eternal mindset, our daily life should change. Faith in the promises of God should radiate through us and put Jesus at the center of our life. He is reflected in all our thoughts and actions. Think of it like this: If we were cut anywhere, Jesus Christ would be seen.

True spiritual wisdom takes our faith in the promises of God and makes them true for each of us. We act on those promises, and our actions produce a fruitful life.

We find a mature sense of satisfaction that comes from spiritual wisdom. This satisfaction is more than just a general feeling of contentment or well-being. This satisfaction comes from believing the promises of God, and finding fulfillment and purpose in those promises. I need to be continually satisfied with the life God has given me in Christ Jesus, with His provision for my daily physical, spiritual, intellectual and emotional needs. I have a God-centered mindset based on my satisfaction in Him.

> **Let them give thanks to the Lord for his unfailing love
> and his wonderful deeds for men,
> for he satisfies the thirsty
> and fills the hungry with good things.**
> **Psalm 107:8-9**

Let's go back to my golf game. If I develop a sense of satisfaction about the game and let my performance flow, I usually do better. I certainly get the most out of my abilities, which may not be a great deal. My satisfaction in the game spreads to those around me and to the other areas of my life.

How's your own golf game? Is satisfaction in God's promises the background for all your relationships? When we're totally satisfied in Christ, we're abandoned to Him. We're like John Wesley: What we know is how we live.

We let our actions, our body, be a temple of the Holy Spirit. He flows through us, transforming us, bringing us from glory to greater glory. Our actions are those of a steward who wants to carry out the work of the master, our Lord.

The great Green Bay Packers coach, Vince Lombardi, encouraged his players to "run with abandonment." As Christians, the only way we can run with abandonment is to be at total peace with the Lord. We surrender all our fears and anxieties. We depend on His sovereignty for our future, His love for our present, His mercy for our past. We focus on our eternal future with Him.

That's not to say we have to have a cheerleader mentality, in which we say "Oh yes, yes!" Running with abandonment is being totally focused on our Lord—our imaginations are the foundation of a God-centered attitude. This attitude is not saying, "I'm not sick," when I really am. A God-centered attitude is saying, "I'm sick, but my sickness is in the Lord's hands and He is my healer!"

> The Lord is near to all who call on him,
> to all who call on him in truth.
> He fulfills the desires of those who fear him;
> he hears their cry and saves them.
> **Psalm 145:18-19**

What a beautiful image: God is near us. He is a God who is close to us on a personal basis. We are engulfed with Him, we are intimate with Him, we feel His presence. We can sincerely and ardently call on Him because we believe He will provide. This forms the foundation for our God-centered attitude.

We have total trust and faith in God. This allows us to live without worry, to live a mindset of godly joy. We have total release from ourselves to love God. Our faith permeates every aspect of our life.

> I have set the Lord always before me.
> Because he is at my right hand,
> I will not be shaken.
> **Psalm 16:8**

Some may say this is a radical attitude to put God emphatically at the center of my life. But I have found there is no other way. With God at the center, joy and peace flow out of me like spokes going out from the hub of a wheel. I am loving, I am thankful. Like all of us, I still struggle with overcoming doubt at times. At those times, I go back to God's Word for encouragement, for guidance, for support, for reassurance, for hope.

Picture throwing a rock into a quiet pond. Waves of water ripple from that one simple act. It's the same with us. Seeking our complete satisfaction in the promises of God has a ripple effect throughout our life.

Let's look at some of the characteristics of God and see how they can affect our life:

A Supernatural God

Imagining God and His ability to create and sustain all the intricacies of the world should cause us to stand in amazement and wonder. How great this God is!

Let's look at a simple structure in the universe—a single cell. The great physiologists may know its minute structure, even down to its different proteins. But they still can't answer all the questions about how it works. They don't know why these proteins behave the way they do, what energizes them, what makes them become signal proteins. Each question leads us deeper into the mystery of its creation. Eventually we come to the fact that no one can answer the final questions: what is God, what is creation, what is man, and what is the single cell?

As a young medical student, I studied single-cell metabolism. Later I thought of myself as a molecular biologist. I even tried to write a book, but realized I didn't know a whole lot about what made the single cell work. I realized the most brilliant scientists don't fully understand even a simple, single cell. That realization was instrumental in leading me to God. The single cell was reason to believe in Him.

God is greater than any of the physical laws of the universe that we know. His power transcends all of our understanding of those laws. By definition, the supernatural transcends the natural and has power over it and isn't limited to it.

Now, some people would try to make God fit into the natural laws He created and be the God of His natural laws. So many great scientists forget any supernatural powers and think only of the power of natural laws, not the supernatural. But author William Lane Craig looks at this concept as a theologian. He says we must look at our God as supernatural, with powers greater than the natural laws, having control over natural laws, but not limited to them or by them.

The supernatural aspect of God gives us freedom from worry and fear. We know He can do all things.

A Merciful Judge

God's mercy is founded upon justice. God is a judge who sits upon the highest throne. His justice is executed upon sin at the cross where Jesus Christ died. His almighty wrath was poured out on the Lord Jesus so that we would receive mercy.

> [All] are justified freely by his grace through the redemption that came by Christ Jesus. God presented him as a sacrifice of atonement, through faith in his blood. He did this to demonstrate his justice.
> **Romans 3:24-25**

A holy God demands judgment for sin. Christ's death on the cross completely satisfied the righteousness of a holy God, making it possible for Him to show mercy righteously. Those who believe, therefore, are treated as righteous because Christ bore their sins.

Through His death on the cross, Christ gives righteousness as a gift to all who come to Him in faith. It is only through Christ's righteousness that we can be declared righteous. The mercy we receive at the cross is founded upon God's justice.

A Loving Heart

Jonathan Edwards talks about love as being one of the essentials of God. Romans 8:32 tells us that His love overflows His sovereignty.

> He who did not spare his own Son, but gave him up for us all—how will he not also, along with him, graciously give us all things?
> **Romans 8:32**

And also in the Gospel of John:

> For God so loved the world that he gave his one and only
> Son, that whoever believes in him shall not perish but have
> eternal life.
> **John 3:16**

This is not an intellectual love. It is the love that desires a relationship with us. The life of King David holds many examples for us of God's love. David had many spiritual ups and downs. One thing he knew, however, was the "father heart" of God. He intimately experienced God's love and forgiveness. Many times he stood in awe and admiration of God's mercy to him.

II Samuel tells the story of David's sin with Bathsheba and his murder plot against Uriah. The prophet Nathan finally helped David see the magnitude of his sins and he confessed: "I have sinned against the Lord" (II Samuel 12:13). Could David ever believe he could be forgiven of his enormous sins? The Lord replied to David through Nathan:

> "The Lord has taken away your sin.
> You are not going to die."
> **II Samuel 12:13**

David knew God's mercy was greater than his own sin. He knew God as his Father, and he knew his Father's heart and his Father's love. Later, David experienced fatherly love of his own when his son Absalom rebelled against him and drove David out of Jerusalem. In the power struggle that followed, Absalom was killed.

> Now Absalom happened to meet David's men. He was riding his mule, and as the mule went under the thick branches of a large oak tree, Absalom's head got caught in the tree. He was left hanging in midair, while the mule he was riding kept on going...[Joab] took three javelins in his hand and plunged them into Absalom's heart while Absalom was

still alive in the oak tree. And ten of Joab's armor-bearers surrounded Absalom, struck him and killed him.
II Samuel 18:9, 14-15

Absalom had sinned cruelly against David. Yet David still loved his son deeply. After Absalom's death, he wept and mourned deeply.

The king was shaken. He went up to the room over the gateway and wept. As he went, he said: "O my son Absalom! My son, my son Absalom! If only I had died instead of you—O Absalom, my son, my son!"
II Samuel 18:33

God shows us that depth of love and forgiveness— the father heart of God.

Our Liberty

When God is our portion, the veil over our hearts is taken away. We have the liberty of the Lord to behold Him with an unshrouded face. Our blindness is lifted, and we are able to come face to face spiritually before God.

Now the Lord is the Spirit, and where the Spirit of the Lord is, there is freedom. And we, who with unveiled faces all reflect the Lord's glory, are being transformed into his likeness with ever-increasing glory, which comes from the Lord, who is the Spirit.
II Corinthians 3:17-18

Our liberty in Christ includes living by the commands of Christ. In Matthew 11:29-30, Jesus Himself describes this as being yoked together with Him, like two oxen pulling a plow. Then He says, "My yoke is easy and my burden is light."

The liberty of knowing our bonds in Christ frees us. We do what we want to do because our bonds are already set in Christ. In Christ we see the transience of the old and we know the glory and freedom of the new.

The New Testament puts a special emphasis on the soul being liberated from the bondage of sin. When we realize we have a position in God, nothing can intimidate us. Nothing can ensnare us. Nothing has a grip on our life but Christ. Christ has liberated us from sin; we can serve Him with fountains of joy.

> It is for freedom that Christ has set us free. Stand firm, then, and do not let yourselves be burdened again by a yoke of slavery.
> **Galatians 5:1**

The only importance of the ceremonial laws and rituals in the Old Testament is that they are pointers to Christ. However, from man-made rules, we are set free. These are the rules that lead to bondage. The heart of faith and the life of liberty lived unto God are our priority.

> For in Christ Jesus neither circumcision nor uncircumcision has any value. The only thing that counts is faith expressing itself through love.
> **Galatians 5:6**

God at Work Through Us

Our godly focus affects all the areas of our life—our emotions, our actions, our relationships, our career, our attitudes. As God loves us, we love others. As God is gracious to us, we are gracious to others. As He is merciful to us, we are merciful to others. As He forgives us, we forgive others. These characteristics of God become ours. They merge and overlap in us and we reflect them to others.

When we let His thoughts be our thoughts, we are filled with a total shalom, a divine peace that leads to imaginations focused on our eternal relationship with Christ.

When I let my mind be filled with imaginations of God, glorifying and worshipping Him, I find joy in my life every day. True joy depends on total abandonment to God and His sovereignty. Christ describes our relationship as joy being made full.

We have a new spirit of joy, of love, of forgiveness, of peace and of generosity. We have new imaginations that transform us internally and change the quality of our relationships with others.

Satan would love to undermine who we are as believers. He would love for us to feel defeated in bad times. He would love for us to be shaky in our faith and forget to focus on God, in good times as well as bad. But Jesus provides our stability. When we feel weak in our faith, we need to look to Him. He will help us regain our strength and stand firm.

> Then Moses summoned Joshua and said to him in the presence of all Israel, "Be strong and courageous, for you must go with this people into the land that the Lord swore to their forefathers to give them...The Lord himself goes before you and will be with you; he will never leave you nor forsake you. Do not be afraid; do not be discouraged."
> **Deuteronomy 31:7-8**

Our strength is not centered on worldly thinking. We have a new vision of God leading us. He is our banner before us, guiding us. Just as He fulfilled His promise to lead the Israelites and give them a new home, He will lead each of us. He is with us, He abides in us, we are engulfed in Him.

Have you faced bitterness, resentment, pride, anger, worry? Each of us must focus on Him and bring our mind into union with His divine knowledge. Seeking the mind of Christ will keep us from self-destruction through our own greed, insecurity, jealousy and other harmful thinking. When Christ is fixed in our thoughts, worldly imaginations can't creep in. We are filled with the Holy Spirit and attitudes that develop from a mind focused on God.

> But the fruit of the Spirit is love, joy, peace, patience, kindness, goodness, faithfulness, gentleness and self-control.
> **Galatians 5:22-23**

The fruit of the Spirit is God at work in us, producing the supernatural qualities of Christ. We cannot develop these qualities fully by ourselves, but only through our union with Christ. Our joy is a joy in Him. Our peace is His *shalom* in our heart.

When we focus on Him in everything we do, we can be filled with positive imaginations. We love others; we're humble; we're cooperative; we're flexible; we work with others rather than against them. We choose constructive solutions rather than destructive criticism.

Think about it this way: We can take a brick and throw it through a window or we can use it to rebuild broken walls. That brick is our attitude. A negative attitude will destroy us and those around us. A positive attitude based on the imaginations of Christ will strengthen us and help us love and appreciate those around us.

Let me share with you a story about Mr. Blancher. Mr. Blancher was serving in the armed forces, stationed in Florida. While there, he went to the library to read books. He noticed one book had many notes written in the margins, and they seemed to be written by someone with great insight and beauty. He read the book in a week, and then re-read it because of the additional comments that enriched his understanding.

He decided to try contacting the writer of the notes. Learning the book had been donated by a woman in New York, he wrote to her and told her how much her notes had meant to him.

Mr. Blancher didn't expect any response. But sure enough, he got one. The two struck up a wonderful correspondence, which continued while Mr. Blancher served overseas. He shared his fears about serving in the war and she comforted him, telling him all great men are scared at one time or another.

She reminded him that the words of the 23rd Psalm told him he could prevail through the valley of the shadow of death. He didn't need to fear because the Lord would be with him and His mighty hand would uphold him.

Mr. Blancher looked forward to her letters because of her strong, thoughtful comments. But he never received a picture of her. He didn't want appearances to affect their relationship. If she were attractive, he was afraid he would continue writing only for her looks. If she were unattractive, he was afraid he would either be just sympathetic to her and quit sharing his thoughts, or that he would lose interest in her.

Finally, Mr. Blancher traveled to New York. He arranged to meet his penpal for the first time at Grand Central Station, followed by dinner. She was to wear a red rose so he could find her in the crowd. When he arrived at the station, he saw this beautiful woman walking toward him. She was more electrifying and alive than he had ever hoped his writer would be. She smiled, then walked past. There was no red rose.

Across the way he saw the woman with the rose. She was about 50 years old, with very conservative clothes and gray hair. She didn't appear to belong in New York. Still, he went over to her and introduced himself. He told her how happy he was to finally meet her and how much he had enjoyed her letters through the years. He said he'd be honored to take her to dinner.

The woman didn't understand. She said a young lady had given her the rose and asked her to wear it. The young lady also said that if a soldier came by and asked her to dinner, she should send him to the restaurant across the street. The young woman would be waiting there.

Sure enough, waiting in the restaurant was the young woman he'd seen in the train station earlier.

Mr. Blancher's focus made the difference in the relationship. He was committed to knowing his letter writer on the inside. He didn't have a negative attitude based on judging the writer's appearance. If he'd thought solely about appearances, he would have been acutely disappointed that the woman with the rose wasn't the beautiful young woman. He might even have decided against approaching the woman with the rose.

Instead, he treasured a relationship with the inner beauty that had been revealed through years of correspondence. He knew that God doesn't judge us by our appearances but by our heart. He sought to do the same. As a result he ended up meeting the beautiful woman after all.

What about us? How often does our attitude reflect the love of Christ? How often are we open to being positive people who focus on Jesus first, and let His love strengthen our relationships with others? Are we inclined to bolster others or battle them? To reassure or resent? To nurture or nag?

To run with abandon, we must be aligned with God. Hebrews 12:2 says, "Let us fix our eyes on Jesus." Our attitude begins with our mind. When we focus first on Christ, a Christ-like attitude will fill us. We are filled with His light. Gone is a spirit of criticism and condemnation. Instead, we are constructive people who believe life is full of God's blessings.

Our perception has changed. No longer do we look at the bad circumstances and events in our life and give in to them. No longer do we wallow in pity, anger, bitterness. We have a new attitude, a new perception and a new hope.

> May the God of hope fill you with all joy and
> peace as you trust in him, so that you may overflow
> with hope by the power of the Holy Spirit.
> **Romans 15:13**

Hope is to the human mind and soul what air is to the lungs. Without hope we can't breathe in our spirits. Hope is absolutely essential to human beings. Our life is dependent upon hope.

We may search for hope in all kinds of ways. It's essential, therefore, that we see the difference between the false hope the world offers and the genuine hope of God.

Genuine hope is based on the promises of God. These promises allow a subjective confidence to grow within us, especially as we read them over and over in His Word. We can feel them being applied to each part of our body.

In certain circumstances we may begin to doubt God's promises. At those times, we need to go back, read His promises in His Word, examine our life to see how He has provided for us in the past, and actually preach to ourselves that the promises of God are true. When our roots are deep into the Word and His promises, we have the eternal hope and strength of God within us.

> For what hope has the godless when he is cut off,
> when God takes away his life?
> **Job 27:8**

Without the resurrection of Jesus Christ, there is no hope for mankind. We are hopeless as human beings. When we accept God's salvation, when He changes our heart, we have a genuine hope—a hope that looks to God, not to the world.

Paul, in writing to his friend and partner in missionary trips, writes of "Christ Jesus our hope" (I Timothy 1:1). Paul reminds Timothy, and each of us, that Christ will help us. He will see us through. He is the embodiment and the personification of hope.

When we have Christ active in our life, we have genuine hope. After all, we live in the eternal hope of God's future grace. He is with us now and forever!

> Always be prepared to give an answer to everyone who asks you to give the reason for the hope that you have.
> **I Peter 3:15**

Our hope is in Christ for our salvation, for our eternity. We are indeed lost if the present time is all we have hope in, all we have hope for. But when Christ, and Christ alone, is our hope, we have hope for all eternity.

When we're worn down, we need to remember that only through Christ do we have hope.

> Why are you downcast, O my soul?
> Why so disturbed within me?
> Put your hope in God,
> for I will yet praise him,
> my Savior and my God.
> **Psalm 42:5**

Hope in God is where we center our mind. We need to constantly remind ourselves, in times of discouragement, to hope in God. When we preach the Word, say the Word to ourselves, we receive the positive reassurance of life—hope!

We know that God is with us. We are focused on His grace, which is with us now and for eternity. We can keep looking for Jesus in all the circumstances in our life and seeking His plan for us.

> May our Lord Jesus Christ himself and God our Father, who loved us and by his grace gave us eternal encouragement and good hope, encourage your hearts and strengthen you in every good deed and word.
> **II Thessalonians 2:16-17**

C.S. Lewis said when we look first at God, we find joy and peace, hope and love. Those imaginations allow us to run with abandon every day. Praise God from whom all these imaginations flow!

Love

I HAVE A SAYING SINCE I BROKE MY LEG: "YOU CAN'T TRUST ANYBODY UNLESS THEY HAVE A LIMP." I CAN LAUGH ABOUT IT. BUT IT REALLY ISN'T ALL THAT FUNNY WHEN I THINK ABOUT IT. MOST OF US ARE MORE INCLINED TO TRUST PEOPLE WHO SEEM FLAWED LIKE WE ARE, PEOPLE WHO LIMP.

All of us are limping spiritually. None of us live without a wounded and handicapped heart. None of us is perfect and flawless. We all have scars that we try to hide or cover up. We all have hearts that can be reluctant to trust—or to love.

Now, we can continue to walk around in this life nursing our wounds, being afraid to completely love and trust others. We can continue to be worried and bitter, angry and resentful, critical and judgmental. Or we can seek healing in the person of Jesus Christ.

> By his wounds we are healed.
> **Isaiah 53:5**

Jesus Christ, who was crucified for us, transforms our heart. His love for us is so great that He died so we may live. He gave up everything so we might fear nothing. His death and resurrection give us a new vision, a new hope, a new world and a new life.

> This is how God showed his love among us: He sent his one and only Son into the world that we might live through him. This is love: not that we loved God, but that he loved

us and sent his Son as an atoning sacrifice for our sins.
I John 4:9-10

We choose how we respond to God's love. We can reject it and continue to live with a wounded heart. Or we can let the imaginations of God's love fill our heart and engulf our life. God's Word tells us the path we should choose:

Love the Lord your God with all your heart and with all your soul and with all your strength.
Deuteronomy 6:5

This verse tells us how much we should love God. Our love should not be merely an intellectual response. Remember the "quickening" John Wesley experienced? He was transformed when he experienced love in his heart as well as in his head.

We can't love God only when it's convenient, when it fits into our schedule or timetable. We must respond with a total commitment to loving Him in all the aspects of our life. We must be abandoned to God in love. Only then, when we surrender completely to God's love, will we receive emotional wholeness.

And I pray that you, being rooted and established in love, may have power, together with all the saints, to grasp how wide and long and high and deep is the love of Christ, and to know this love that surpasses knowledge—that you may be filled to the measure of all the fullness of God.
Ephesians 3:17-19

Paul's beautiful description helps me imagine God's love—a love that is incomprehensible in its depth and breadth and length and height.

Christ's love is beyond measure. Its **depth** is demonstrated by how far down He reaches to save each of us. The story of Manasseh in the Old Testament gives us just one example. Manasseh became king at age 12 and was a detestable king.

He restored all the practices of idolatry his father, Hezekiah, had demolished. Finally, he is captured by the Assyrians, who carried him prisoner to Babylon.

> In his distress he sought the favor of the Lord his God and humbled himself greatly before the God of his fathers. And when he prayed to him, the Lord was moved by his entreaty and listened to his plea; so he brought him back to Jerusalem and to his kingdom. Then Manasseh knew that the Lord is God.
> **II Chronicles 33:12-13**

God reached down to save Manasseh at the lowest point in his life, after he had committed reprehensible sins against God. He will reach down to us, no matter how far away from Him we feel.

Hear how **wide** Christ's love is, how it extends to all people:

> With your blood you purchased men for God
> from every tribe and language and people and nation.
> **Revelation 5:9**

The **length** of Christ's love may be compared with how He goes through all our trials with us, supporting and upholding us.

> We are hard pressed on every side, but not crushed; perplexed, but not in despair; persecuted, but not abandoned; struck down, but not destroyed. We always carry around in our body the death of Jesus, so that the life of Jesus may also be revealed in our body.
> **II Corinthians 4:8-10**

The **height** of Christ's love is described by how high He brings us—to the right hand of God, to the throne of God, to be intimate with Him as His bride forever in heaven.

But you have come to Mount Zion, to the heavenly
Jerusalem, the city of the living God. You have come to
thousands upon thousands of angels in joyful assembly, to
the church of the firstborn, whose names are written in
heaven. You have come to God, the judge of all men, to the
spirits of righteous men made perfect, to Jesus the media-
tor of a new covenant, and to the sprinkled blood that
speaks a better word than the blood of Abel.
Hebrews 12:22-24

We should stand in awe of the immeasurable love of
Christ! The Christ who redeems us. The Christ who saves us.
The Christ who lives in us and transforms us.

We should focus our imaginations on how much He loves
us and how much we love Him. We should seek a life filled
with constant imaginations of "this love that surpasses
knowledge." We should respond to God's love by living a life
of love.

Be imitators of God, therefore, as dearly loved children and
live a life of love, just as Christ loved us and gave himself up
for us as a fragrant offering and sacrifice to God.
Ephesians 5:1

The love that God gives us we are to give to others. A life
of love is not love directed merely at God. Instead, we must
direct God's love, as it flows through us, to others.

Dear friends, let us love one another, for love comes from
God. Everyone who loves has been born of God and
knows God. Whoever does not love does not know God,
because God is love.
1 John 4:7-8

If anyone says, "I love God," yet hates his brother, he is a
liar. For anyone who does not love his brother, whom he
has seen, cannot love God, whom he has not seen.

And he has given us this command:
Whoever loves God must also love his brother.
I John 4:20-21

I think loving others gives us an inward glow and makes us truly beautiful. I saw two sisters the other day. The first one said of the second, "She's the pretty one." The second one replied, "Oh, no. She's the pretty one." They were both gorgeous and they were teasing each other. And they are both beautiful inside and out. The inner glow made them physically beautiful. Letting love spread is an essential imagination of the mind.

Loving others isn't always easy. Author C.S. Lewis says that to love is to take a risk, to be vulnerable, to reveal ourselves to another being. With our wounded human heart, we can be reluctant to take that risk. On the other hand, to be totally secure and without risk means loving nothing and no one. If we risk little, we lose little. But we also gain little out of life.

Hear the words of Jesus as He quotes the prophesy of Isaiah:

For this people's heart has become calloused;
they hardly hear with their ears,
and they have closed their eyes.
Otherwise they might see with their eyes,
hear with their ears,
understand with their hearts
and turn, and I would heal them.
Matthew 13:15

God has shown us a better way. He has taken the risk for us. He loves us so much that He let His son die on the cross for us. He has given with complete abandon. He is ready to heal us. No longer will we be people who limp! We are perfect through His grace.

And He wants us to have the same attitude: to give in an abandoned way to all people. He doesn't want us to love others with a selfish motive. God's love is not self-serving. He wants us to accept the risks associated with loving and give those risks to Him. He will take care of the sufferings that occur because we love and care for others. He wants us to love without thought to the consequences.

There is no fear in love. But perfect love drives out fear.
I John 4:18

God's love is complete and pure; it is perfect. It is the love that drives out the fear of rejection and humiliation we associate with the risk of loving others. We don't need to guard against being hurt, thereby setting limits on our ability to love.

Instead, we can love with abandon, casting all our cares and anxieties on Him, freeing us to love others even more. This is the love that satisfies. This is the love that fulfills. This is the love that transforms. This is the love God taught us through the sacrifice of His Son. May we share His gift through our love.

The Strong Foundation

ARE YOU A JEALOUS OR ENVIOUS PERSON? OR CAN YOU REJOICE IN A BROTHER'S SUCCESS? DO YOU ALWAYS DESIRE TO GET EVEN? OR DO YOU PRAY FOR TOTAL FORGIVENESS OF THOSE WHO HAVE HURT YOU? ARE YOU MORE CONCERNED ABOUT HELPING YOURSELF THAN HELPING OTHERS? ALL THESE ATTITUDES BOIL DOWN TO A CENTRAL QUESTION: WHO DO YOU LOVE FIRST, CHRIST OR YOURSELF?

Relationships are the basis of life. That's why it's so important to have healthy, lasting, loving relationships with all those around us. So many of our imaginations stem from the quality of our relationships. And the key to successful relationships is our relationship with the Lord.

The Old Testament tells us the story of the relationship between two friends—David and Jonathan. These two had the perfect harmony of the attributes of God flowing between them. Their love produced grace, grace produced mercy and mercy produced forgiveness.

Jonathan did not share his father's prejudices against David. David did not hold it against Jonathan that he was loyal to his father and remained with his father, even though Saul was opposed to David. They knew each other and knew each other's heart. Most of all, they both knew the heart of God.

Like David and Jonathan, we will find such peace in relationships only when we enter a complete and loving relationship with the Lord and then are able to share His love with others.

Jesus needs to be in every relationship. With Him as the foundation of our relationships, we are people who intercede for others. As in marriage, we must work to give and forgive, otherwise selfishness will destroy the relationship. We are intercessors when we are in God's spirit.

Relationships are critical in our life! I see people who achieve so much and accomplish so much, but who forget to work in their relationships with others. They may have some superficial relationships, but they have none with real substance. This is really a shame. Relationships are what make life so rich and rewarding.

Let me tell you about a doctor who formerly worked at St. Luke's. He specialized in relationships. He made patients feel great and special. He had this little smile and twinkle about him that gave a lift to everyone. Now he didn't have the kind of worldly success others had. But he did well. He even was president of the Pennsylvania Ophthalmological Society.

More important, he knew that monetary rewards would never be completely satisfying. And he knew that people who look only for worldly success will never be happy. But doctors who view medicine from the perspective of how much good they can do for their patients will have a different kind of success—true satisfaction. And that he had!

I think it's easy for people who are loving to others to love Christ. They build strong relationships with people because they have an open heart and are willing to trust others. But those who have trouble loving people will struggle to love Christ. Relationships don't come easily to them, and it's difficult to trust and surrender to the Lord if it's difficult to trust others.

We need to exercise God's love, His grace, His mercy, His forgiveness in our life every day. We cannot allow ourselves to be spiritual couch potatoes, who take in from the Holy Spirit but never give back to others. We want to have all the spiritual strength there is by loving others, showing grace and forgiveness and mercy.

Storge

Many people think of romantic love just as a sexual relationship. And if there isn't a sexual relationship, or it has diminished, then they think love is gone. There's an essential ingredient that makes the difference between relationships that are lasting and relationships that are fleeting—affection.

C.S. Lewis, in his book *The Four Loves*, calls this form of love *storge*, which means "respect, caring for, encouraging." It is an affection that mingles with the other loves—friendship, erotic love and the love of God. Imaginations of affection strengthen our relationships.

The mindset of *storge*, as C.S. Lewis says, is so important. Without it, we lose the joy and the spirit that God wants us to have.

All the relationships of life that are void of *storge* are not loves, but are unloves. *Storge*—affection, encouragement, an appreciation for others—is an essential part of all true love relationships.

With affection, we're interested in more than experiencing a sexual relationship. We appreciate our spouse, we respect our spouse, we want to give to our spouse more than we want to get something in return. When the affection becomes paramount then *eros* becomes true love.

Erotic love without affection is just the opposite of love— it's selfishness and greed. We enter a relationship to get something for ourselves—a source of security or a source of sexual gratification. But when affection combines with *eros*, then true love grows.

There's a story about a great trader who lived on a faraway island. The time came in his life when he was ready to get married and settle down. The custom in that part of the world was for men to choose a wife and pay the family a dowry. The size of the dowry depended on how much the girl was worth. A beautiful girl was worth five or six cows. An unattractive girl was worth just one cow.

The trader could choose any girl he wanted to be his wife. Finally he decided and approached the girl's father. Now, most people, including the father, knew the girl was really only worth one cow. But the trader saw special qualities in her. He saw she was a radiant person with great potential. He offered her father a dowry of eight cows! The father accepted, thinking that he had gotten quite a bargain.

In the next five years, the trader encouraged the best in his wife. He appreciated her, reassured her and loved her. The woman became one of the most remarkable on the island.

Well, the father came back to the trader. "You cheated me," he said. "You didn't give me enough cattle for my daughter. She's worth 10 cows, at least." The father finally realized the true value of his daughter.

The husband and wife just smiled. They realized their relationship was built on appreciating and encouraging each other. They knew that their relationship was what made each of them special.

This is what *storge* is all about. We appreciate, care, support, encourage and have affection for others so they live up to their full potential.

> If we love one another, God lives in us and his love is made complete in us.
> **I John 4:12**

Affection transforms our relationship with others and gives it greater meaning. *Storge* is a selfless love interested in the good of others, so we no longer worry about ourselves. We treat others with dignity and respect. *Storge* sees the good in others and dwells on the positive. We anticipate the other person's desires and interests and we seek to meet those needs in deference.

Storge also transforms our relationship with God. No longer do we have a formal relationship with lip service, but we have a vital, deeply personal and intimate relationship. We have constant appreciation for God, valuing and esteeming Him above all else. We see Him as incomparable. We appreciate Jesus so much that we don't need the appreciation of other human beings. At the same time, we abandon ourselves to God, relinquishing everything to Him. *Storge* focuses on God's glory—praises, worships and adores Him.

Storge is often misunderstood. Some people have never received unconditional love and they don't feel, within themselves, that they are adequate. Some people think they have to do something to earn another person's approval. Some people have trouble showing affection. They think they have to give something extra to others. They can't just be themselves and relax. Others may give their bodies to overcome their feelings of inadequacy.

Affection is one of our basic needs. God calls us to be His friends, not just His servants. The affection He feels for us is something we must feel deeply. God loves us and has made everything possible for us.

When we feel His affection, we can pass that love on to others. It gives us an enduring life because when we're full of appreciation, we're filled with love and kindness. *Storge* gets rid of the worry and bitterness and critical spirit in our life. We are no longer determined to find the bad in situations and people.

When we focus on *storge*, our relationships are fueled by the eternal fire of God's love. We respect others, we encourage others, we appreciate others and we love others.

Marriage

Be honest with yourself. What do you think about your relationship with your spouse? Answer honestly. Not what you tell other people, even your spouse, but what you really think. Is it a good relationship or a bad one? Would you marry your spouse again or would you rather not be married to your partner? Are your feelings growing positively or negatively?

Let's look at marriage for a minute because I think it's the most dominant relationship of life.

Some people come into marriage based on sex. Others have built a foundation with friendship, commitment, appreciation and godly love. This relationship then leads to sex.

For followers of Christ, love between a man and a woman should be centered in Christ. The *agape* love of Christ was shown for each of them. And each of them should show that love toward the other. This concept of love is foreign to many people. How blessed is the couple who have surrendered their hearts to Christ!

Do you look at your spouse as God's gift to you? Do you look at God first or your spouse first? The role Jesus has in this relationship says much about the role He has in the rest of our relationships and the rest of our life.

When I wake up every morning, I ask Jesus to be in each part of my wife. I ask God's blessings for Heather each day. I bless her so that Jesus is in her mind and her eyes and her heart, so that she thinks and sees and loves as Jesus does.

Respect, character, friendship, affection and enjoyment are the basis of a good marriage. Two people who marry should understand each other, love each other and care for each other. In marriage, and in all relationships, we can be truly happy if we're thankful and have an appreciative heart for one another.

There's one more area of imaginations that is especially critical to the health of a marriage—fantasies.

Many married people struggle with fantasies about other people. Some may act on those fantasies and pursue relationships outside their marriage. Or the fantasies may stay just that. The person may remain true to his or her spouse. Others may use their fantasies to generate excitement in their marriage, pretending their spouse is the person about whom they fantasize. And still others may try to deny, even to themselves, that they have fantasies.

All of us have fantasies. Some writers have said that men struggle with them more than women do, but I think all of us face this problem to a greater or lesser extent. None of us is perfect when it comes to our own intimacy. We can't ignore fantasies and hope they go away. We must be honest and admit our weaknesses. If we truly want to have a Christ-like mind, we have to deal with fantasies in a way that will glorify God.

First, we should not be surprised that believers struggle with fantasies. However, we are still under the provision of God's grace because we have faith in Him through Jesus Christ.

Therefore, there is now no condemnation for those who are in Christ Jesus, because through Christ Jesus the law of

the Spirit of life set me free from the law of sin and death.
Romans 8:1-2

Second, we must remember we are not alone. God has given us the Holy Spirit to guide us, even as we deal with fantasies. The Holy Spirit can empower us to direct the fantasies toward our spouse. The Holy Spirit can strengthen us when we feel tempted to act.

We can do more than simply say, "I'm not going to give in." We can relinquish our struggle, and let the Holy Spirit guide us and protect us. And we can let that desire be filled and complemented with a desire for God—a desire to love God, to be committed to God, to know God. The best plan is to find God in everything, and to even make our intimacy part of our relationship with Him. Then we can let that desire strengthen our marriage.

I think part of the problem is frequently we take sex too seriously and marriage not seriously enough. The priority here is that we make marriage a lot of fun, but also recognize its great importance and significance.

Now, this doesn't mean that sex should be solemn and serious. In a committed, Christian relationship, sex should be a joyous time when people are together: they can talk, they can pray, they can enjoy being themselves.

Some people are so serious that they can't be affectionate. Some people are so serious they can't laugh and enjoy each other. Or they're so worried about being important or pious.

Sex is a joyous gift from God that should be enjoyed. It can, and should, include laughter that doesn't degrade, but simply relaxes and promotes enjoyment. We should laugh and rejoice in our relationship with one another and with the Lord.

Loving Jesus, Loving Others

LET'S FACE IT, IN ANY RELATIONSHIP WE'LL STRUGGLE WITH RESOLVING CONFLICT. WHEN WE ARE FOCUSED ON JESUS, WE CAN BE LOVING. WE CAN PUT THE OTHER PERSON FIRST, WE CAN LISTEN, WE CAN BE HUMBLE AND WE CAN GIVE. CONFLICT WILL NEVER GO AWAY. BUT WE'LL HAVE THE TOOLS TO RESOLVE PROBLEMS RATHER THAN LETTING THEM FESTER AND DESTROY THE RELATIONSHIP.

Without Jesus, we put ourselves first and will eventually destroy our relationship. Here are some ways that happens:

• We seek recognition from other people rather than finding contentment in serving God. I know people who will go out of their way to be recognized for something that has no real meaning.

There are others who want to look so good that they adopt bad business practices, such as altering their books, so they will appear successful. They deceive others so they feel better about themselves.

• We blame others for our own problems. For example, some people who have trouble with their hearing won't always admit it's their problem. They blame others for speaking too quickly or too slowly, too loudly or too softly. Some who are unhappy in their marriage seek to blame it on their spouse. So they look for other relationships, thinking a different person will make them happy.

If we're not careful, we find it too easy to blame others for our own shortcomings. Or we prize the love and approval of others more than we should. If our life is marked by seeking others' approval or blaming others, we haven't found true contentment in Christ.

• We want to control the relationship and make the other person give us what we want. There are many reasons for doing this. By controlling, the controller feels more important and powerful. In controlling, one person tries to manipulate the other. Frequently the relationship disintegrates because the controlling nature of one person prevents a truly balanced relationship from forming. Then the one thing the controlling person wanted—a relationship—is gone.

Now, there's a better way to guide others. It's the Socratic way of asking questions, which imparts knowledge without being controlling or manipulative. We can ask such questions as, "What are the consequences of your behavior?" The questions determine the best decision to a situation. And it's the opposite of trying to control another's thoughts and actions. It's a great way to guide a child, or others in personal or business relationships. Yet it takes time, tenderness and imagination.

Underneath these attitudes is the belief that says we don't need God. We're good all on our own. In our selfishness, we become self-righteous. We're people who don't rely on God's spirit. We disapprove of the sin—and the sinner.

We can see the underlying attitude that "we don't need God" by the way we treat others. Saul of Tarsus exemplified self-reliance. He hated Stephen, a man full of faith and the Holy Spirit. Acts 8:1 records that Saul gave approval to Stephen's death. Saul was a very harsh, uncaring man. He was self-righteous and didn't think he needed God. Later, he was humbled, and after encountering Jesus, Saul became the great Apostle Paul.

On the other hand, in the Lord Jesus we constantly see love for others, particularly the sinner. Jesus surprised the self-righteous Pharisees by his direct, clear love for sinners.

The story of Zacchaeus beautifully portrays Christ's love for the unlovable.

When Jesus reached the spot, he looked up and said to him, "Zacchaeus, come down immediately. I must stay at your house today." So he came down at once and welcomed him gladly.

All the people saw this and began to mutter, "He has gone to be the guest of a 'sinner.'"
Luke 19:5-7

Zacchaeus was a notorious swindler in the community— a traitor to the Romans; taking taxes from the Jews. The Lord Jesus told Zacchaeus He was going to his house, completely shocking the Pharisees with the idea that He would be the guest in a sinner's home.

How evident is the Lord Jesus' beautiful spirit toward sinners. He is compassionate and interested. He truly is the model for all our relationships.

We can hate sin, but we are called to love the sinner. We are called to pray for the sinner, including our own sinful ways. We are called to intercede for others—to pray for each other.

Now, it's not always easy to be an intercessor. There are times when others are difficult to deal with. They may be filled with anger or worry or cynicism, among other things. But our response is to love them and pray for them. We need to be filled with the Holy Spirit, praying for those who use us, hate us and act against us.

The Rev. Larry Jackson, from North Carolina, says we must pray from the position of the person for whom we are interceding. We use our imaginations to put ourselves in that person's position. If that person is in a state of disarray, we must put ourselves in that state and pray as they would. From that position, we often find ourselves awake to God, feeling the turmoil and grief of the person as we pray for him or her.

Each of us has gifts from God. How do we use these gifts in our relationships? Do we use them to build up others in a spirit of intercession and righteous truth? Or do we use them to build up ourselves, by criticizing, judging, admonishing, condemning or telling others what to do? Do we seek the truth at all costs, or do we temper our actions and thoughts with our imaginations of a loving God? Are we critical of others, admonishing and correcting them? Or do we build others up, appreciating and thanking them?

It's easy to slide into deluding ourselves, denying our struggles. We rationalize, we lie, and we say all sorts of things that are misleading, especially to ourselves. That's why it's essential to be brutally honest with ourselves, admitting our struggles.

We also need accountability with other people of the same sex. We must take the next step and admit our struggles to someone else. God made us to share each other's burdens. It becomes a much lighter load when the load is shared.

The principle of accountability and being responsible is a great help to us. It helps us to keep focused on a desire to honor God and to say, "Thy will be done," even when something is unpleasant to us.

Let's say one of our children opens the car door in a parking lot, damaging a gold Porsche parked in the next slot. We go to all lengths to find the owner of the Porsche to make the situation right. We may not do this with overflowing joy, but we do it from a desire to honor God. Along with our action comes peace and a sweetness to submitting to God's difficult providences, and doing what's right.

This is part of Christian maturity. It's shown in very practical circumstances, such as picking up trash scattered from our curbside can during the night by the neighborhood cat! We probably aren't elated with a sense of privilege, but we do what's right out of a desire to honor God.

God knows how to bless those actions. He knows how to give a peace and sweetness to saying, "Thy will be done." So being responsible is another motivation to live by that God uses to direct us through unpleasant circumstances.

Before long we discover God uses these occasions in ways that surprise us. Then we will thank Him for the circumstances and rejoice to have such an overruling God in all the details of our life. Ultimately it comes back to a desire to honor the Lord Jesus in any situation.

Our heart must be tuned to God. Then we are pliable through His love so we can love others. When we focus our mind and thoughts on the person of Jesus we are not accusers. We're filled with His love. Let's focus on Jesus Christ so others can see Christ through us.

Delusion of Reprieve

HOW OFTEN HAVE YOU PUT OFF HAVING TO DEAL WITH THE CONSEQUENCES OF YOUR ACTIONS, HOPING THE PROBLEM WILL SORT ITSELF OUT OR JUST GO AWAY? THERE'S A FALSE IMAGINATION AT WORK HERE—A DELUSION SATAN USES TO KEEP US SEPARATED FROM GOD. I CALL IT A "DELUSION OF REPRIEVE." WE HOPE GOD WILL JUST SMOOTH PROBLEMS OVER AND THAT HE WON'T HOLD US ACCOUNTABLE FOR OUR THOUGHTS AND ACTIONS.

How very wrong this thinking is! Yet we've all had times in our life in which we've hoped God would give us a reprieve from the consequences of our actions. I've gone into exams having done things other than study the night before the test. Then I would ask God to give me wisdom, knowledge and discernment. But lo and behold, I didn't do well on the test. I wonder why! Was my faith insufficient? God could have taken care of me. He could have made me smart when I hadn't studied. But He didn't. Instead, He held me accountable for my actions.

I am accountable to God for the way I treat anyone with whom I do business. I must always ask myself how the Lord would treat that person if He were in my shoes. I'm also accountable for the more than 300 employees at St. Luke's. If I hurt those people or if I am responsible for them turning away from the Lord, I am held accountable. I'm responsible for everyone who works for me.

I'm also accountable for my thoughts. It's not enough to act in a way that honors and worships and obeys God. For each of us, our thoughts must also be focused on Him. We must let His mind be our mind. To think we can lust, just because we don't commit adultery is a delusion. It is a delusion to think these thoughts are OK. The Bible says our imaginations of lust are just as wrong as the actions of adultery.

> You have heard that it was said, "Do not commit adultery." But I tell you that anyone who looks at a woman lustfully has already committed adultery with her in his heart.
> **Matthew 5:27-28**

One of my friends confronted a gentleman who went to church but who was living a lifestyle that was outside Christ. He told my friend, "Oh, don't worry about it. I'm just a carnal Christian."

He had the imagination of himself as someone who was saved, but he wasn't living under the lordship of Jesus Christ. He accepted God's grace, but he was indifferent to his responsibilities in living a life for Christ. He wasn't living under the premise that God is sovereign. His mindset was preventing the Holy Spirit from abounding in him. This gentleman needed to ask himself, "Does Christ really mean anything to me?"

How often are we indifferent to our responsibilities in living a life for Christ? Are there times when we think He will forgive us and we'll be OK, regardless of how we live?

Now, certainly, we trust in God's grace—the power of His resurrection over our sins and every area affected by our sins. We know that God is sovereign and we can trust in Him to meet our daily needs. But the fact that the Lord forgave us for our sins doesn't mean we don't have to go to work in the morning to provide food for our family.

We must guard against a delusion of misunderstanding God's grace. The wrong attitude is saying: "I don't have to worry about anything, God will take care of everything." "I don't have to worry about building up bad debts because God will take care of me." "I don't have to worry about not taking care of my physical health because His grace will take care of me." "I don't have to worry about being spiritually and ethically correct, because God's grace will cover all my sins."

Grace does indeed cover the sins of those who have a living trust in Him. Praise God that He is so merciful to us! But His grace doesn't excuse us from living in a way that responds to Him. We need to be fiscally responsible. We need to be responsible for our physical body, making sure we're living a healthy lifestyle. We need to be responsible for our mind, staying mentally sharp. And we need to be responsible in all our thoughts and actions, which should be aligned to Him.

We cannot intentionally continue to sin and rely on an assumption about God's grace. In essence, we're lying to ourselves. We're trying to convince ourselves that God doesn't need to be in control of every area of our life. John Owen, who is considered by many to be one of the greatest Puritan theologians, once said, "Be sure of this and let it be fixed in your mind, that if you do not repent of this secret sin you are engaged in, you will perish forever."

Owen, like many Reformed theologians, believed wholeheartedly in God's sovereignty in salvation. God's grace is indeed sufficient for all our sins. But Owen also emphasized our human responsibility to live out our faith with a transformed heart and mind.

Let's go back to the example of adultery. Say someone who claimed to be a Christian was living in adultery. Some people would say they were saved when they "made their decision for Christ" and they can never be lost, even though they may ruin their family. They might even use the expression, "once saved, always saved," to support their opinion.

This is an incomplete teaching. We are saved by the blood of Christ AND a changed heart that continues to fight the fight of faith to the end.

> **Therefore, if anyone is in Christ, he is a new creation; the old has gone, the new has come!**
> **II Corinthians 5:17**

Just because someone makes a profession of faith doesn't mean they have experienced a saving change in their heart. Our life must back up our words. It is a Christian's joy to be firmly trusting in the heart of God, engulfed in the Trinity, interwound with the person of Christ, living in His pure and perfect love and grace. Grace is such a beautiful aspect of life. It's a shame to cheapen it by not putting Christ in everything we do or not totally abiding in Him for everything.

Unfortunately, at times we are unwatchful and play with sin, biting on Satan's lures. We can get complacent. We think we can sin just this one time because we've been faithful in the past. In those times, we need to hear God's Word.

> So, if you think you are standing firm, be careful that you don't fall!
> **I Corinthians 10:12**

At other times, we may feel weak in our faith and sense that sin is greater than we are. God does not let us struggle alone, as Paul writes in the next verse.

> No temptation has seized you except what is common to man. And God is faithful; he will not let you be tempted beyond what you can bear. But when you are tempted, he will also provide a way out so that you can stand up under it.
> **I Corinthians 10:13**

As our Father and Savior, God will help us. This verse points out the perfect balance of grace and responsibility. God's sovereign faithfulness will provide, and we must continue to repent and believe in His grace.

We cannot take a profession of faith as a guarantee that we are saved and always will be. Every day we must persevere in the fight of faith.

Jonathan Edwards explained it this way: "That there is a real difference between them that fall away and them that persevere…[they fall away] because they have no root in themselves; because they have not counted the cost; and because they have no oil in their vessels. Those who have no root differ from those who have root. Those who have oil differ from those who have no oil."

The Bible teaches that those who enter heaven must persevere in the fight of faith. "He who stands firm to the end will be saved," Jesus says in Matthew 10:22. We must "fight the good fight of the faith" (I Timothy 6:12). Our responsibility is to continue in faith, for without faith there is no relationship with the person of Jesus Christ.

We will be presented holy in heaven by Christ, "if you continue in your faith, established and firm, not moved from the hope held out in the gospel" (Colossians 1:23).

To persevere, we must take action.

> If your right hand causes you to sin, cut it off and throw it away. It is better for you to lose one part of your body than for your whole body to go into hell.
> **Matthew 5:30**

Sin destroys our claim to have true faith. Sin is contrary to the principle of faith. When we are flirting with temptation, we must remember God's promise in Deuteronomy and repeated in the book of Hebrews:

> Never will I leave you;
> never will I forsake you.
> **Hebrews 13:5**

God vows to be with us and to provide the divine help we need. He is behind the scenes to revive our faith and our sense of repentance. Consider these promises:

> Though he stumble, he will not fall,
> for the Lord upholds him with his hand.
> **Psalm 37:24**

> But the Lord is faithful, and he will strengthen and protect you from the evil one.
> **II Thessalonians 3:3**

Remember, these promises are made to those who believe. If there is no faith, we cannot claim the promise. True faith, and true salvation, is to be forgiven and to be a new creature in Christ—with a transformed life of faith. We must have a saving union with Christ that makes a difference in our life.

If we believe He won't hold us accountable for our thoughts and actions, we begin to think, "Maybe I don't need God. I can be independent and do what I want because it doesn't matter to God." We no longer live by faith. We no longer live according to the mind of Christ.

Dr. James D. Smith, in a lecture on the laboratory of the mind, said, "When there is a sin in our lives, we have told ourselves the Lord doesn't care about this area of our life. This is an imagination of the mind that is a lie."

Lying to ourselves is so dangerous! We may try to deceive ourselves, but we can never deceive God. He knows our heart. He knows our thoughts. He knows our mind. Sin will separate us from God. We will never be able to fully focus our imaginations on Him when lies create a chasm between us.

Have you ever said certain things and acted a certain way around one group of friends, and then said other things and acted differently with another group? All of us may do this to some extent: say certain things on the golf course, act a certain way when we're playing bridge, and then act differently around the dinner table with our family.

But this behavior gets dangerous when there's a definite break between who we are in one group and who we become in a second group. I've known people who love to be with the "in" crowd on Saturday night, and then come to church to worship on Sunday morning. Sometimes there's a smug attitude that surrounds all this: "I'm getting away with something while others are living by simple rules." The two halves are not integrated. They're kept in separate boxes inside a person's mind. They think their behavior doesn't affect anyone. But this is false thinking. It's a delusion to think we can divide our attention and our actions. In reality, this behavior hurts everyone.

In its most extreme form, a delusion of reprieve is the mindset for non-believers. This mindset says the Bible is not true. The Word of God is not true. We don't believe God will hold us accountable because we don't believe in Him and don't love Him. We think we can get by with living a life outside of Christ.

One of the greatest men I know is a lawyer. He doesn't do anything wrong; in fact, everything about him is good. He's tall, good-looking, respected in the community and in his profession. But he doesn't believe the Bible or in Jesus Christ. He thinks all he needs are good actions. He is probably less sinful on the outside than any man I know.

But he won't be able to find his place in God's heaven because he thinks that everything he needs to do is external. He may be a great lawyer and a good person, but these are all outward manifestations. They don't come from a relationship with Jesus Christ. Until he really loves Jesus, and has true faith that Jesus is the basis of his existence, he's suffering under the delusion of reprieve. This man, as good as he is, will go to hell rather than spend eternity with the living God.

What a dangerous attitude! If we don't believe in God and His Word, we're telling God to go His way and we'll go ours. We don't believe that we're sinners. We're telling Him our independence, our sinful life on earth, is more important than His truth and His eternal life.

There are many people who carry this attitude into their living. Unlike my friend, they're not necessarily seeking to be good people. They treat people the way the world treats them. They think that's the way life is. They're not honorable. They aren't kind and loving. They're bitter, angry, resentful, worried, self-centered and destructive. When they make decisions, they don't consider the eternity beyond the grave. Thus, they make superficial decisions that cost them dearly, taking them further from the heart of God.

The truth is that we matter to God. More than that, we are His children! He loves us. He cares about our thoughts and actions. He cares about how we choose to think and what we choose to do.

We must come under the convictions of our sin, and then we must believe in His grace to redeem us. So often people have a hard time believing they're sinners—the delusion of reprieve. Or some don't believe God's grace is enough. They think have to earn redemption. We can get caught on either one of these points and not really rise to the joy of being saved by His grace. We must be clear on this point: God calls us to persevere in the fight of faith by His grace.

When we are tempted to walk away from our faith we must ask ourselves whether we choose Christ or choose sin. If we choose sin and don't repent, we will perish.

Our faith is nourished by secret springs that are not known to the world. Every day we must thank God that our faith is sustained by the heavenly intercession of Christ for us.

Because I live, you also will live.
John 14:19

In *The Pilgrim's Progress* there is a wonderful image of how Christ sustains our faith. Christian is shown a fire in front of a wall. A man is pouring water on it, yet the fire grows higher and hotter. He doesn't understand why the fire won't go out. Then he is shown the other side of the wall, where he sees One secretly pouring oil into the fire.

The fire is the grace of God in our heart. The man with the bucket of water is Satan, trying to drown out our faith. Behind the wall is Christ, who is sustaining the faith of the believer with the oil of the Holy Spirit.

What a powerful image to fix in our mind! We don't need to live in the fear of perishing because of sin! God supports us and keeps us strong. We live in loving gratitude to Christ for interceding in times of temptation. He will strengthen us. We are never alone!

A Forgiving Spirit

HAVE YOU EVER BEEN FALSELY ACCUSED BY SOMEONE? HAS ANYONE EVER HURT YOU—INTENTIONALLY OR BY ACCIDENT? WHAT SHOULD YOUR IMAGINATIONS BE IN THOSE CIRCUMSTANCES? DOES FOCUSING ON JESUS AFFECT YOUR ATTITUDE?

Look at Jesus' life and death. Imagine Him looking down from the cross at His tormentors. He was exhausted and broken, pain seared His body. Yet, He wasn't hoping for some miracle to save Him. He wasn't angry. He wasn't plotting His revenge.

Hear His words:

> Father, forgive them, for they do not know
> what they are doing.
> **Luke 23:34**

Jesus, in His death and resurrection, seeks God's forgiveness not just for those who plotted against Him and killed Him.

He seeks forgiveness for all of us. All of us are sinners. We all struggle with sins created by our own selfishness.

> If we claim to be without sin,
> we deceive ourselves and the truth is not in us.
> **I John 1:8**

But God does not leave us in this sinful state.

If we confess our sins, he is faithful and just and will forgive us our sins and purify us from all unrighteousness.
I John 1:9

None of us can deny that we sin. But when we believe in the cleansing blood of Christ's death and resurrection, we are freed from sin. Christianity is the state of forgiveness. God forgives us. He purifies us. He saves us through Jesus Christ.

Here is a trustworthy saying that deserves full acceptance: Christ Jesus came into the world to save sinners.
I Timothy 1:15

Our mind needs to focus on Christ's loving sacrifice for us. Jesus, as God, gave up His rights. He died on the cross for us, even though we didn't deserve such a loving action. God did not turn us over to death as punishment for sin. He forgave us completely—and died the death we should have died. Through His sacrifice, we received everything—eternal life!

That's the beautiful image of forgiveness I like to hold in my mind: Jesus' forgiveness as complete, unqualified, unconditional giving of self.

Yet receiving and believing in His forgiveness is only one side of the coin. When we experience His limitless forgiveness of us, we're able to forgive others. We act out His forgiveness of our sins by forgiving others. My satisfaction in His perfect forgiveness allows me to be forgiving in relationships with others.

Let me give you an example. Let's say a friend says something unfair to me. So I replay the events in my head and get angry. Instead of recognizing this vain imagination, I nurse along my bad feelings. Instead of focusing on Jesus' forgiveness to me and extending that forgiveness to my friend, I begin to savor my anger. I let thoughts of revenge and retaliation fill my mind. I start to feel tense and stressed out and even exhausted.

Soon, Satan has a stronghold in my mind; I am filled with death, not Christ's overflowing life. My entire perspective is distorted and I become useless to the Lord. I cannot function as a man of God, for I am filled with sin-filled imaginations because of my inability to forgive.

I could have stopped that scenario. And I should have. I should have asked God for help. I should have thanked Jesus for His sacrificial forgiveness and the power to channel that forgiveness to my offender. I should have prayed for deliverance from the evil thoughts and rebuked Satan. I should have meditated on God's love for me and His promise to never leave me or forsake me. I should have, I should have, I should have.

It's all up to me. I choose what thoughts fill my mind. I choose my own attitude. Do I choose anger, resentment and bitterness? Do I let my desire for revenge distort my thinking and do I spread lies and malicious gossip? Or do I choose forgiveness, as I have been forgiven? God's Word is explicit in its instruction.

> Get rid of all bitterness, rage and anger, brawling and slander, along with every form of malice. Be kind and compassionate to one another, forgiving each other, just as in Christ God forgave you.
> **Ephesians 4:31-32**

The Lord is gracious to us, and we need to be gracious in return. Forgiveness is to the spirit what exercise is to the body. We're given a body, and if we don't exercise it, we become couch potatoes. We're given Jesus Christ and His forgiveness, and if we don't forgive others, then we become spiritual couch potatoes. We can either be captives to bitterness and anger because we don't forgive others, or we can embody the forgiveness of Christ.

When we pray, we should ask God to "forgive us our debts, as we also have forgiven our debtors" (Matthew 6:12). Why should we ask such a thing? Jesus explains:

> For if you forgive men when they sin against you, your heavenly Father will also forgive you. But if you do not forgive men their sins, your Father will not forgive your sins.
> **Matthew 6:14-15**

Jesus tells a parable recorded in Matthew that illustrates this point. Jesus says the "kingdom of heaven is like a king who wanted to settle accounts with his servants." One servant, who owed the king a great deal of money, was unable to pay his debt. The king ordered that the man and his family be sold to pay the money. But the servant pleaded with the king, and the king canceled the debt and let the man go.

Yet the servant went to another servant who owed him a small sum of money and demanded to be paid. The fellow servant begged and pleaded: "Be patient with me, and I will pay you back." But the man was unmoved and had the other servant thrown in jail. When the master heard about the incident, he called the servant before him.

> "You wicked servant," he said, "I canceled all that debt of yours because you begged me to. Shouldn't you have had mercy on your fellow servant just as I had on you?" In anger his master turned him over to the jailers to be tortured, until he should pay back all he owed.
> **Matthew 18:32-34**

Jesus tells us the lesson to learn:

> This is how my heavenly Father will treat each of you unless you forgive your brother from your heart.
> **Matthew 18:35**

Forgiveness is crucial in all our relationships. Otherwise, resentment, bitterness and anger fester. We build up defensive walls. We deny the hurt and try to convince ourselves that everything is OK.

But that only deepens the wound. We damage the dynamic nature of our relationships by running from conflict and pain. Our relationship, especially a marriage or close friendship, will be destroyed.

The vain imaginations that stem from an unforgiving heart will also destroy us physically, mentally, emotionally and spiritually. We're filled with stress, anxiety and depression. Our blood pressure rises. We can get ulcers and weakened physical health. It's not worth the risk to hold bitterness and resentment in our heart.

All of us have been wronged by others—by lies, by stealing, by gossip and so on. After all, no one is perfect, not even our friends and loved ones. And when we're wronged, there are times when we'd rather respond with anger and resentment. Let me share an example from my own life.

As I grew up in the coal fields in West Virginia, I found out that if I didn't do my best, I'd be picked on. I didn't prove to be a great competitor or warrior, but I acquired the habit of always hitting back. I always carried a grudge if anyone did anything against me. I always remembered the wrong they did to me. It's hard to play in the dirt without getting dirty.

I reached a point in my life where anyone who harmed me received a double payback. I was very angry and resentful. I was pulled down mentally, spiritually and emotionally. It damaged my ability to enjoy life.

As I grew closer to the Lord, I realized how much these attitudes hurt me. They hurt my life, they hurt my relationships with others, and they especially hindered my relationship with the Lord.

I had to confront my anger. I had to realize these attitudes were sinful and let them go. I had to refuse to let myself get caught up with anger and resentment and hatred. I had to acknowledge these emotions were the worst possible response.

And then I had to learn to forgive. When I forgave others and let go of my anger, I was dramatically changed. Forgiveness empowered me to become strong in my relationship with the Lord. I developed a closer relationship with God, which gave me joy, peace and inner calm.

See to it that no one misses the grace of God and that no bitter root grows up to cause trouble and defile many.
Hebrews 12:15

Bitterness, anger and resentment cause us trouble and defile our relationship with God. They can only be cured by receiving God's grace and mercy for healing. Then we are truly able to forgive, and, if necessary, confront the situation in love. Jesus is the source of our forgiveness.

When Christ is the focus of our thoughts, we no longer harbor selfish attitudes that make us unforgiving and judgmental. Our mind is freed from the grudges, bitterness and anger we experience when we have been wronged.

As human beings, there are limits on our own ability to forgive. But through the love and forgiveness enacted on the cross—Christ's sacrificial and self-emptying love and forgive-ness—we can love and forgive others.

Only through our imaginations of Christ can our mind be freed from the bitterness and resentment that keep us from forgiving others.

Forgiveness is an act of unconditional love—one of our greatest images of Christ. When we forgive others, we relin-quish our rights as the one sinned against, and we choose to not demand recourse or retaliation. We release our offender to God. We turn the situation over to Christ, for He's the one who will right all the wrongs. All we can do is pray for those we think have offended us. Our prayers will change us. As I have prayed for my offenders, I have been changed. I have learned that I need to care for others. And I have grown closer to Christ.

When forgiving someone, it's also important to be specific—so specific that we could write down the attitude or event we need to forgive. We can't generalize specific acts so they become wholesale assaults on character. It's difficult to forgive someone "for being bad."

Instead, we need to forgive what they do, not who they are. We pray for the sinner, but we dislike the sin and refuse to let it become part of our life. We no longer regard the offense as a debt owed to us.

> Do not repay anyone evil for evil. Be careful to do what is right in the eyes of everybody. If it is possible, as far as it depends on you, live at peace with everyone. Do not take revenge, my friends, but leave room for God's wrath, for it is written: "It is mine to avenge; I will repay," says the Lord.
> **Romans 12:17-19**

The world teaches us that the correct response when someone hurts us is for us to hurt them back. So often, when we want to be mean, angry or hurtful to others, we are destroyed by our anger and our attempts to hurt others.

God teaches us that the best response is total forgiveness. The receiver of our forgiveness may not deserve it, according to the rules of the world. But God loves that person as He loves us. His forgiveness is free to all who accept it. His response, therefore, should be our response. The greatest forms of forgiveness repay evil with kindness, giving love when there is no reason to love and no guarantee that love will be returned.

> Then Peter came to Jesus and asked, "Lord, how many times shall I forgive my brother when he sins against me? Up to seven times?"
>
> Jesus answered, "I tell you, not seven times, but seventy-seven times."
> **Matthew 18:21-22**

I'm sure Peter thought he was being very generous when he suggested the number seven. He probably was overwhelmed when Jesus countered with such a high number. But I don't think Jesus intends for us to keep count. He wants us to be people with a forgiving nature. We must release the offense as often as needed.

One practical way to do this is to say to ourselves, "I forgive this offense (being as specific as possible) in Jesus' name." We can repeat that until it's part of our innermost being. Then we have the power of Christ in us, guiding our forgiveness.

Now, repeated forgiveness should not be confused with tolerance. Forgiveness is not a license for the offender. We must be intolerant of evil. Yet we can still forgive. And let the Lord take care of the rest.

This attitude of forgiveness takes a lot of faith in Christ's love. We have to choose by faith to offer this kind of forgiveness. The apostles responded to Christ by saying, "Increase our faith!" (Luke 17:5) We have access to an unlimited source of faith because we have experienced Jesus' sacrificial death of forgiveness. It is His forgiveness that is channeled through us to others. God is in us and works through us.

When we make forgiveness one of the major aspects of our life, we are free from the bondage of resentment and anger. Total forgiveness results in total freedom. A mindset of forgiveness clears the way so we can focus more fully on Christ. Our thoughts aren't cluttered with bitterness and resentment. We are filled with imaginations of joy, peace and love—blessings we receive from our Lord, Jesus Christ!

A Life of Caring

WHAT DO YOU EXPECT OUT OF YOUR RELATIONSHIPS? IS IT BETTER TO GET AS MUCH AS YOU CAN? OR DO YOU TRY TO SERVE THE OTHER PERSON?

Before we can apply any imaginations to our relationships with others, let's look at God's attitude toward us.

C.S. Lewis says there's a parallel between creation and redemption. God didn't need to create us. He did it for His own enjoyment, to have a relationship with us. The same is true of redemption. He didn't need to give us Jesus as a Savior. But He did it because He wanted to restore the relationship with His people. God's free and giving heart made Him first create us and then later redeem us. It is His nature to give and love. It's not based on anything in us.

While the world looks to get and be filled, God is already full. He looks forward to giving. He wants to give us His love, His blessings, His riches, so we, in turn, can be channels of His abundance to others.

When our mind finds satisfaction in God's promises, we find His free and giving heart reflected in our own attitude. We give to others freely. We are less concerned with what we receive and with having our own needs met. We are less concerned with hoarding what God has blessed us with. After all, we know that God will satisfy us and always provide for us.

> Remember this: Whoever sows sparingly will also reap sparingly, and whoever sows generously will also reap generously. Each man should give what he has decided in his heart to give, not reluctantly or under compulsion, for God loves a cheerful giver.
> **II Corinthians 9:6-7**

I had an aunt who loved to be pampered. She would stay in bed until 10 o'clock every morning. She spent her days always wanting a little more than she had. She was never satisfied. Now, she had the nicest husband in the world, but I don't think she ever appreciated him. She was busy wanting more from life. She ended up dissipated and dying. I'm not sure she ever found satisfaction from life.

On the other hand, I can't imagine life without giving. I love to give of myself, not only with money but also by giving of myself in my profession and my community. I never want to retire and just sit around all day. I find the greatest satisfaction in serving others and want to be a servant the rest of my life.

Let me share with you another story.

A mother was cleaning up the kitchen one evening when her 14-year-old son ran through and into his bedroom. He slammed the door and threw himself on the bed. His mother went into the room to see what was wrong, but he wouldn't talk to her. He just buried his head under the pillow and refused to acknowledge her presence. She sat there for a few minutes, but got no response. So she went back in the kitchen and waited until her husband got home. She was concerned because she'd never seen her son this upset.

When her husband arrived, she told him what had happened and how concerned she was. He went to talk with his son. In a gentle, quiet voice he asked his son how he was doing. No response. "Did you go out with your girlfriend tonight?" The son hesitantly said yes. The father asked if the son had done anything wrong. The son abruptly answered no.

Then they began to talk about whether the son and the girlfriend loved each other. As the two—father and son—talked, it became clear that the girl loved the boy more than the boy loved the girl. That was what was bothering him. He didn't really care for her, but he realized he was capable of using her for his own enjoyment.

Well, the father was troubled. It's difficult to help children, as they grow, to discover their feelings and attitudes and help them handle those emotions responsibly. So the father and son talked about the difference between using a person for selfish gain or truly giving to a person because you care about him or her.

This dynamic occurs in all kinds of relationships—in business, in politics, between parents and children, between those who are attracted to each other. As the father told his son, "It's quite easy to take people and get them to do things for you, even if you don't care for them." It's easy for some people to form friendships with people of importance so they can find success in politics or business. It's easy to get in the habit of finding mutual attraction and using that to fulfill your own wants and desires without caring for the other person.

We discussed the antidote earlier—*storge*. When there is mutual caring, love and appreciation, we ensure that we're not abusing a relationship. We genuinely care for others, so we look to serve them first.

Our imaginations of the mind should make us realize we are to be caregivers—loving others and serving others.

And let us consider how we may spur
one another on toward love and good deeds.
Hebrews 10:24

The essence of life is serving others. If we focus all our energy on ourselves, we frequently find many disconcerting and covetous thoughts—anger, envy, lust and other imaginations that never give us peace. When we think of ourselves rather than others, we're never satisfied, and we seldom find true, purposeful activity.

For even the Son of Man did not come to be served,
but to serve, and to give his life as a ransom for many.
Mark 10:45

Jesus calls Himself the Son of Man about 80 times in the New Testament. This term gives us a rich image of Him as the representative for all of us. Other terms reveal different aspects of His nature. Son of God, for instance, reveals His divine nature.

But as the Son of Man, Jesus serves. The implication, therefore, is that as Jesus serves others, so should we. If the Son of Man is a servant, so should all men and women be servants.

And serving is a great delight! It puts our whole being in perspective and it provides one of the greatest forms of healthy imaginations. If we're focused on others, we have little time to think of our own needs. We can't imagine that we aren't satisfied if we're trying to satisfy others.

> Therefore, as God's chosen people, holy and dearly loved, clothe yourselves with compassion, kindness, humility, gentleness and patience. Bear with each other and forgive whatever grievances you may have against one another. Forgive as the Lord forgave you. And over all these virtues put on love, which binds them all together in perfect unity.
> **Colossians 3:12-14**

In these verses, Paul spells out the imaginations we must have as God's children—imaginations that guide us as we serve others. These are attitudes that will always put others first and help us effectively care for others in our daily life. Not all of us will be professional caregivers, but all of us should care for others because God loves us.

Serving others helps us fight selfish imaginations. It's difficult to be proud when we put others first. It's difficult to be filled with anger when we have imaginations of forgiveness. It's difficult to worry when we're filled with patience through the Holy Spirit.

We must be able to love others in order to care for them. We must submit to them so we can care for them.

> Do nothing out of selfish ambition or vain conceit, but in humility consider others better than yourselves.
> **Philippians 2:3**

Caregiving allows us to grow deeper spiritually. When we care for others, we take on their burdens by praying for them.

It actually makes us stronger, too. As we serve others, we come closer to God. When we are focused on the Lord as we serve, we glorify Him. We don't act for our own glory.

Romans 12 offers some guidelines for serving. Eugene H. Peterson, in his exciting version of the New Testament called *The Message*, offers it this way:

> If you're called to give aid to people in distress, keep your eyes open and be quick to respond; if you work with the disadvantaged, don't let yourself get irritated with them or depressed by them. Keep a smile on your face. Love from the center of who you are; don't fake it. Run for dear life from evil; hold on for dear life to good. Be good friends who love deeply; practice playing second fiddle. Don't burn out; keep yourselves fueled and aflame. Be alert servants of the Master, cheerfully expectant. Don't quit in hard times; pray all the harder. Help needy Christians; be inventive in hospitality.

Paul offers many tips, but also some warnings. If we try to take on others' burdens and handle it ourselves, we will self-destruct. In all things, we must be servants who are full of God's love, or we will be destroyed.

There is a triangle of service. Christ is the foundation; those who serve and those who are being served are the sides, submitted to each other and to Christ. In marriage, husband and wife are the sides. In an occupation, employer and employee are the sides. We come together to love each other, serve each other and serve others, doing His work.

Whatever we do, no matter how good it is, won't amount to anything unless Jesus is in it. Only when we have Jesus permeating us will our acts be of value. We need to do His work in His name, by the power of the Holy Spirit living within us.

Our whole life's work is to pursue the Lord's purpose for our life. In our mind we are to find God's goal and pursue it. We have to ask the Lord for His purpose for our life.

The best attitude we can bring toward our work is to enjoy it, to feel it is where we belong and to see it as our ministry, as doing the Lord's work regardless of the job. It has been said that the happiest person you know will be the one who is happiest at his occupation. Most people who are happy at their work are happy with themselves. The two go hand-in-hand.

People who have God's spirit in their work and in their life have a spirit of cooperation, harmony and enjoyment.

This is the key difference between two friends of Jesus, sisters named Mary and Martha. Martha was busy working around the house, getting ready for Jesus' visit. On the surface, it seemed like the right attitude to have. She was preparing for the Lord because she loved Him and wanted Him to be comfortable during their time together. But let's look more closely at her attitude when Jesus arrived.

> But Martha was distracted by all the preparations that had to be made. She came to him and asked, "Lord, don't you care that my sister has left me to do the work by myself? Tell her to help me!"
> **Luke 10:40**

Did Martha find peace in Jesus' presence? Was she happy to be with Him? It doesn't seem that way. She appeared to be more concerned about how much she was doing. Even more, she was concerned about how little her sister was doing. She was proud of her accomplishments and critical of her sister. And she wanted Jesus to side with her and tell Mary to get moving.

How would you respond? Here's what Jesus said:

> "Martha, Martha," the Lord answered, "you are worried and upset about many things, but only one thing is needed. Mary has chosen what is better, and it will not be taken away from her."
> **Luke 10:41-42**

Actions matter less than attitude. It was important that Martha prepared the house and cared for the guests. But more important was her attitude. While Martha was scurrying around, Mary was sitting at Jesus' feet, listening to Him. Martha was "distracted by the preparations." Mary was focused on Jesus and looked to Him.

It's the same with us. Jesus sees through our work to the inner attitude that directs our actions. He knows when the Holy Spirit is guiding us and when our own desire for praise or success is directing us.

Our work must be guided by God's spirit, rather than our own. When we try to work under our own power, we're focused on worldly measures and worldly standards of success. We become tense in our work, we burn out in our attitude toward our work, and we can let our work destroy our physical health.

There's that good kind of tired feeling when we've put in a productive day's work. We feel we've been useful. But if we try to do too much or carry that feeling too far, then we're exhausted. I constantly ask the Lord to teach me not to do any work because of myself. My strength is renewed when I am resting in my relationship with Him. I know I cannot do His work solely through my efforts. He must lead me. His strength supports me.

> Let us not become weary in doing good, for at the proper time we will reap a harvest if we do not give up.
> **Galatians 6:9**

When we work with the Spirit of the Lord guiding us, Jesus blossoms forth in us. We have His joy, His peace, His eternal vision leading us. When we live in His energy and His power, we have great peace and great activity. We have His equipping power guiding us in our work, allowing us to act without the distractions of this world. We can focus on our work through Him, with His ease and patience, and we experience joy in work.

Now, it's easy to think we are doing what God wants us to do, yet still miss the mark. The test is whether we are enjoying the work or whether we are anxious and worried about the work. Do we do the best we can and not worry about the rest? When we call ourselves Christian and work to do the things of Christ, we must let Him take charge. We must abide in His presence.

Do we ask Jesus to be in our business and career decisions? As we buy and sell, do we ask Jesus if that is what He would have us do? Is it greed or godly thinking that motivates our choices?

Many people in the workplace tend to think they have to worry about the attitude of others around them, their working conditions and other external circumstances. Now certainly these factors have their influence on our ability to perform our job. But more essential is how we focus our mind at work and what we allow ourselves to be concerned with.

We need to make wise decisions for Jesus, decisions that honor and glorify Him. May our decisions show we have truly been crucified and that Christ lives in us.

A Mind of Faith

GOD IS SO GREAT WE CANNOT FULLY COMPREHEND HIM. AND WE UNDERSTAND VERY LITTLE ABOUT EARTH, LET ALONE HEAVEN. SO HOW DO WE THINK WE CAN TRULY TAKE ON THE MIND OF CHRIST? HOW CAN WE UNITE OUR MIND WITH HIS?

Our faith in God's grace enables us to enter into a deeply personal and intimate relationship with Him. With imaginations of faith we enter God's mind of grace and we are in union with Him.

God's grace is revealed in the faith of believers in the Old Testament and the New Testament. For example, God's grace was at work in the life of Abraham, who believed he could have a child at age 100; who believed he could go out in faith from his people and form a new group of people to be God's people; who believed those people would cover the earth.

Let's look again at what the Bible teaches us about God, about faith and our relationship with our Creator, Redeemer and Sustainer.

> Great is the Lord and most worthy of praise;
> his greatness no one can fathom.
> **Psalm 145:3**

Consider the complexity of a single cell. There's an irreducible complexity in the single cell that cannot be understood. For those of us who have been out of biology class for a while, a cell is a very small unit of protoplasm, usually with a nucleus and an enclosing membrane.

All plants and animals are made up of one or more cells. No one understands all the mechanisms of a single cell or how to make one. As I mentioned earlier, when I studied the cell's complexities as a medical student, I knew there was a God. I experienced my own personal "quickening." All doubt was gone as I saw physical evidence that could not have occurred by chance or evolution, but had to be intelligently designed.

I realized the mind that had designed that one single cell—so simple yet so complex—was greater than any human mind could even begin to understand.

There is an irreducible complexity also in the stars and the stratosphere that truly can't be understood, let alone designed by man. Astronomers now realize that the universe has more than a dozen evenly distributed clumps of galaxies. One of the clumps of galaxies closest to the earth measures 500 million light years long, 200 million light years wide and 15 million light years thick. In case your high school astronomy has grown fuzzy, a light year is a little less than 6 trillion miles! And He calls the stars by name while He listens to our heart's cry! What a God he must be!

> Praise the Lord.
> How good it is to sing praises to our God,
> how pleasant and fitting to praise him!
> The Lord builds up Jerusalem;
> he gathers the exiles of Israel.
> He heals the brokenhearted
> and binds up their wounds.
> He determines the number of the stars
> and calls them each by name.
> Great is our Lord and mighty in power;
> his understanding has no limit.
> **Psalm 147:1-5**

God's understanding is without limit; it is infinite! "Infinite" means extending beyond measure or comprehension; endless; immense; inexhaustible. This Psalm tells us that

God's understanding is as vast as the stars that He calls by name, but as intimate as knowing each person's innermost needs.

There's an irreducible complexity in the integration of both the small and large in everything we see. Even the greatest minds in physics cannot explain how all the physical laws integrate together in the beautiful manner that is absolutely required for coordination of the universe and for life to exist.

This irreducible complexity of both the small and the large, and the integration in between, tells us there must be some person, some mind, that was in the beginning who had the knowledge to create everything—because He knew everything.

In today's world of technology, we have achieved incredible feats. Our inventions are awesome. But with all our ingenuity, we still cannot create something from nothing. Only God can!

The mind of God is to be worshiped and reckoned with in our lives as we understand that we are not the wisdom of the age—we are the product of the wisdom of the age!

> God's voice thunders in marvelous ways;
> he does great things beyond our understanding.
> **Job 37:5**

It takes a wise person to look at the complexity of a single cell or of the entire universe and realize there must be a God. Faith does not abandon natural reasoning. Faith says, "There is a scientific relationship to God that exists with what we can't see."

> By faith we understand that the universe was formed at
> God's command, so that what is seen was not made out of
> what was visible.
> **Hebrews 11:3**

Faith cannot be explained by natural laws. We can understand those laws, but we also realize we can't explain life or eternity. In the irreducible complexity of all life we acknowledge God's awesome power—power that is beyond what we see, what we understand, what we comprehend.

Think about the relationship between a husband and wife. While the partners don't always understand each other, they trust each other. Their trust brings about true intimacy.

It's similar to our relationship with God. We may not understand God fully, but we trust Him, we have faith in Him, and our hope is in Him.

Now faith is being sure of what we hope for and certain of what we do not see.
Hebrews 11:1

We live by faith, not by sight.
II Corinthians 5:7

This is the essence of faith—believing beyond what we see and understand. And trusting in God, the Creator of all.

Now, we can look at the universe and marvel at the power of God. We can believe in that power. But our faith isn't activated until we believe in another kind of God's power: the power of the resurrection. God is so powerful, not even death could stop Him!

There is a reason for this amazing demonstration of power. This is the greatest expression of love in the universe: the agreement of the Father and the Son for Christ to be sacrificed on the cross as an atonement for our sin.

For God so loved the world that he gave
his one and only Son, that whoever believes
in him shall not perish but have eternal life.
John 3:16

He died on the cross so that every sinner who trusts in Him will find complete forgiveness for all their sins.

Here is a trustworthy saying that deserves full acceptance:
Christ Jesus came into the world to save sinners.
I Timothy 1:15

Through His death and resurrection, we receive eternal life!

> I am the resurrection and the life. He who believes in me will live, even though he dies; and whoever lives and believes in me will never die.
> **John 11:25-26**

> I tell you the truth, he who believes has everlasting life.
> **John 6:47**

This is the matchless grace of God! This is God's pure and perfect mind of grace. The climax of God's mind of grace is seen on the cross, when Jesus took all our sins upon Himself and said, "It is finished." His merciful redemption—His grace—saves us.

> For it is by grace you have been saved, through faith—and this not from yourselves, it is the gift of God—not by works, so that no one can boast.
> **Ephesians 2:8-9**

What is our response to such an overwhelming gift of love and grace? Should we be arrogant, thinking we don't need grace? No! All of us are sinners in need of this grace. We must wipe out our self-righteousness and live the life of faith. There is nothing more basic to the Christian life than a conscious sense of our daily need of Christ.

We cannot earn God's grace, for we all are sinners. Instead, we must believe in a God who is merciful and who has love, grace and mercy for those who are in Him.

Our only response should be to accept this gift—to surrender ourselves to God and to be born again by God's grace and by His spirit.

> Jesus answered, "I tell you the truth, no one can enter the kingdom of God unless he is born of water and the Spirit."
> **John 3:5**

Faith goes beyond the power we see exhibited in creation. Faith is an unconditional commitment to our Lord that brings our mind to His mind. Faith is a relationship with God—a relationship that begins when we believe in Him and draw near to Him.

> Come near to God and he will come near to you.
> **James 4:8**

"Near" is being aligned to God, being satisfied with Him and enjoying Him. These attitudes of affection strengthen our relationship with God. We are engulfed and interwound with Him. Ours is a dynamic and dramatic relationship!

> May [Christ] dwell in your hearts through faith. And I pray that you, being rooted and established in love, may have power, together with all the saints, to grasp how wide and long and high and deep is the love of Christ, and to know this love that surpasses knowledge—that you may be filled to the measure of all the fullness of God.
> **Ephesians 3:17-19**

This is the God who created a single cell and the vast universe! This is the Almighty, who loves us so much He let His Son die on the cross!

We are filled with faith in the unseen fullness of God. We experience His eternal love and eternal life. We experience *metanoia* through our unconditional faith in His grace. We are born again as the children of God!

> Therefore, if anyone is in Christ, he is a new creation: the old has gone, the new has come!
> **II Corinthians 5:17**

We are God's created people. When we look to Him with our mind of faith, we are engulfed and intimately entwined with His mind of grace. We can't comprehend His wisdom, but we can believe His promises.

And this is what he has promised us—even eternal life.
I John 2:25

The promises of God change people, and change people's minds, so they can be at one with God's mind of grace.

But by the grace of God I am what I am, and his grace to me was not without effect. No, I worked harder than all of them—yet not I, but the grace of God that was with me.
I Corinthians 15:10

Now, we will become spiritual couch potatoes if we don't live out our mind of faith and God's mind of grace. For example, we have been forgiven by God. Therefore, we must forgive others. Just as our physical body becomes a couch potato if we don't exercise, we will become a spiritual couch potato if we don't practice forgiveness.

Our purpose in life is the opposite of a couch potato. Our purpose is to live out our transforming faith in His grace. Our mindset and our actions will tell us when we're on the right track—when we find true satisfaction in Him.

We glorify God most by being aligned with His mind of grace, being satisfied with Him, having faith in Him and enjoying Him. We find true contentment in Him. We find a sense of love, of well-being, of delight, of hope and of anticipation. We have no desire for anything other than Christ!

We live before an audience of one—our Lord and Savior, Jesus Christ. We are totally satisfied in Jesus, with no wants for what this world offers. We are sublimely at peace with God. What He has, whatever He gives satisfies us. All we do is ask every day what God wants, and then do what God wants.

Our sense of satisfaction glorifies God. We enhance God's glory when the way we live calls attention to His majesty. We don't make God better; we simply make His greatness more apparent to others. To display the glory of God should be our purpose in everything.

This is to my Father's glory, that you bear much fruit, showing yourselves to be my disciples.
John 15:8

We integrate eternity into our life every day when our sense of satisfaction glorifies God. He is our portion, and we are filled with peace, joy, thanksgiving and love.

This is the true effect of our thoughts on our life. How we think now affects our eternity! There is so much to live for in godly imaginations.

DO WE ENACT OUR HOPE IN GOD SO WE HAVE JOY AND POWER? DO WE LIVE OUT THE COMMANDMENTS OF GOD SO WE'RE SANCTIFIED? DO WE HAVE PEACE BECAUSE WE BELIEVE IN HIS FUTURE GRACE? DO WE HAVE POWER BECAUSE WE ALLOW THE HOLY SPIRIT TO RUN US INSTEAD OF US TRYING TO RUN OURSELVES? DO WE ALLOW ALL OF THIS TO CHANGE OUR LIFE?

These mental attitudes are very important for a changed life. We must enact in life what we know to be correct: the Word of God in our mind and as seen in the person of Jesus Christ.

Why are our imaginations so important? Listen to this advice from the Apostle Paul:

> Do not be deceived: God cannot be mocked. A man reaps what he sows. The one who sows to please his sinful nature, from that nature will reap destruction; the one who sows to please the Spirit, from the Spirit will reap eternal life.
> **Galatians 6:7-8**

Our fate for eternity hangs in the balance. If we have godly thoughts, we reap godly blessings now and always. If we have earthly thoughts, we reap an unfulfilled life full of the sins that stem from selfishness. Our sinful nature, left unchecked, will destroy us. We'll never find perfect peace, joy and love through the imaginations of this world.

Consider, then, the rich blessings of the Lord. The moment we surrender to Christ, we're engulfed and empowered by the Holy Spirit. We're translated from the temporal to the eternal. We reap everlasting life with the Creator of the universe. What greater harvest can there be?

Our thoughts now are the building blocks that determine how we live in eternity. Are we surrendered to Christ? Then we seek Him every day. Are we focused more on the diversions of this world, the fleeting pleasures that money and success can buy? Then we will spend eternity without Him.

Let me tell you about a friend of mine, Jamie Buckingham. At first, Jamie had trouble accepting that he had cancer. For a year and a half, through tests and operations and various medical procedures, Jamie kept asking God what he was supposed to learn from all this. Jamie waged a valiant battle against cancer and enjoyed a series of miracles against the disease. And then he died.

But before he died, Jamie understood. He knew the Lord was saying it was time for the two of them to get closer. Jamie was released from the fear of death because he walked closer than ever to the Lord. He told how he was no longer concerned with the church, his writings and other priorities that had previously been so important. He was completely tuned to God's presence because he was stripped of worldly concerns of life. There no longer was all the clutter of daily life, the obligations, activities and agendas of the world. It was just Jamie and Jesus. Jesus and Jamie.

> Therefore we do not lose heart. Though outwardly we are wasting away, yet inwardly we are being renewed day by day. For our light and momentary troubles are achieving for us an eternal glory that far outweighs them all. So we fix our eyes not on what is seen, but on what is unseen. For what is seen is temporary, but what is unseen is eternal.
> **II Corinthians 4:16-18**

God wants us to be spiritually one with Him, appreciating that He created us, and that He desires to be one with us for eternity in our mind and in our existence. Our life's purpose is to live with Him and not by ourselves. Our union with Him includes the perfect plan for our life. The Lord God is with us and in us throughout the day. We never tire of beholding His great, irreducible complexity in creation. We stand in awe of His love, His great beauty, His great saving grace through His Son who gave up everything for us!

This is the reason we live! Those who find it, find the richest of all blessings now and forever—Him.

God says, "I will be with you all the time. I will make sure every minute of life is filled with what is best for you, the most interesting for you, the most rewarding for you, and that you will leave knowing you did absolutely the best."

We have to be with Him by knowing Him, becoming like Him, serving Him and being in eternity with Him. At the end of our life, we will be judged not for what we did, but whether we did it within a relationship with Christ; whether we did it with His love, His peace and with imaginations of Him.

This exclusive imagination of being with Him requires a great deal of focus that is strengthened through Bible study, prayer and relationships with other believers. Any time we let worldly imaginations enter in, we become vulnerable to drifting away from Him. We can lose the purpose of life by becoming preoccupied with imaginations of the world rather than imaginations of God.

Our purpose in life is to see whether we can be totally sold out to Christ, because our attitude today determines our attitude for eternity.

We need to seek that goal of completely honoring Him daily. We need to give ourselves to Him cheerfully and joyfully. We need to give our work to Him. We need to give our money to Him. We need to give our all to Him.

The Westminster Catechism says, "The chief end of man is to glorify God and enjoy Him forever."

God wants us to glorify Him and enjoy Him forever. He wants us to be totally focused on Him. We must have a mind-set that we will glorify our eternal partner forever. We glorify Him by worshipping Him. That worship starts at the cross, where we bow and receive His forgiveness for our sins from the risen Lord Jesus. We surrender ourselves to Him. Then we can enjoy the person of Christ, our Creator, now and forever. Nothing separates us from Him.

Author John Piper says this in a slightly different way. He writes, in his book *Future Grace*, "The chief end of man is to glorify God by enjoying Him forever." This is the essence of imaginations that are filled with eternal faith in the grace of our Lord.

> Since, then, you have been raised with Christ, set your hearts on things above, where Christ is seated at the right hand of God. Set your minds on things above, not on earthly things. For you died, and your life is now hidden with Christ in God. When Christ, who is your life, appears, then you also will appear with him in glory.
> **Colossians 3:1-4**

Our ultimate imagination is to glorify God by enjoying Him! There is nothing other than the person of Jesus, because in the person of Jesus all things are centered and around Him all things revolve. He is our portion in life. He is our eternity. He will do far more than we can think and comprehend—exceedingly and abundantly so! His power will work in us to bring glory to God through us—His people, the church. He is the most wonderful imagination of the mind! Amen and amen!

EPILOGUE

WHEN YOU WAKE UP IN THE MORNING, DO YOU WAKE UP HAPPY? DO YOU WAKE UP WITH JOY IN YOUR HEART? DO YOU WAKE UP WANTING TO LIVE THIS DAY WITH ENTHUSIASM? DO YOU WAKE UP WITH THANKSGIVING? DO YOU WAKE UP WITH LOVE? THE ATTITUDE WE HAVE EVERY MORNING DETERMINES THE ATTITUDE WE WILL HAVE FOR ETERNITY.

Let's review the three basic premises of this book:

- **We are what we think, and what we think is what we act.** We have imaginations, then thoughts, actions, habit and character. We really become who we are as a result of our thoughts.

- **God is most glorified in us when we are most satisfied in Him.** We must truly surrender to the satisfaction of being with Jesus and letting Him provide for us. This mindset frees us from daily worry and concern. Our relationship with Him is the foundation for all our thoughts and actions. It replaces negative attitudes with positive imaginations based on Christ, filling us with peace, joy and love. And it allows us to be effective for Him.

- **Our thoughts now set the tone for how we'll spend eternity.** When our thoughts are faithfully focused on God, we'll be rewarded in eternity. We have an initial glimpse of eternity now, and we will be richly rewarded in His presence in heaven.

NOTES

S C R I P T U R E I N D E X

James P. Gills, M.D., is founder and director of St. Luke's Cataract and Laser Institute in Tarpon Springs, Florida. Internationally respected as a cataract surgeon, he has performed more cataract extractions and lens implantations than anyone else in the world. He has pioneered many advancements in the field of ophthalmology to make cataract surgery safer and easier.

As a world-renowned ophthalmologist, Dr. Gills has received innumerable medical and educational awards, highlighted by three listings in the *Best Doctors in America*, including 1999. Dr. Gills is a clinical professor of ophthalmology at the University of South Florida, and was named one of the Best Ophthalmologists in America in 1996 by ophthalmic academic leaders nationwide. He serves on the Board of Visitors at Duke University Medical Center and the Advisory Board of Wilmer Ophthalmological Institute at Johns Hopkins University. He has published more than 135 medical papers and authored eight medical textbooks. Listed in *Marquis Who's Who in America*, Dr. Gills was Entrepreneur of the Year 1990 for the State of Florida, received the Tampa Bay Business Hall of Fame Award in 1993, and the Tampa Bay Ethics Award from the University of Tampa in 1995. In 1996 he was awarded the prestigious Innovators Award by his colleagues in the American Society of Cataract and Refractive Surgery. In 2000 Dr. Gills received the Merchants Association of Florida Enterprise Medal, an award given to outstanding entrepreneurs who give back to their community, Humanitarian of the Year Award, presented by the Golda Mier/Kent Jewish Center, Free Enterpriser of the Year Award from the Florida Council on Economic Education; and Philanthropist of the Year presented by the Suncoast Chapter of the National Society of Fund Raising Executives. In 2001 the Salvation Army presented Dr. Gills with their prestigious Others Award.

Dr. Gills has dedicated his life to restoring much more than physical vision. He seeks to encourage and comfort the patients who come to St. Luke's. It was through sharing his insights with patients that he initially began writing on Christian topics. An avid student of the Bible for many years, he now has authored 12 books dealing with his personal commitment to Christ and physical fitness.

As an ultra-distance athlete, Dr. Gills participated in 46 marathons, including 18 Boston Marathons and 14 100-mile mountain runs. In addition, he completed five Ironman Triathlons in Hawaii and six Double Iron Triathlons. Dr. Gills has served on the national Board of Directors of the Fellowship of Christian Athletes and in 1991 was the first recipient of their Tom Landry Award.

Married in 1962, Dr. and Mrs. Gills are very proud of their family. Daughter Shea, a retired attorney, and husband, Shane Grundy, M.D. are parents of three children, twins Maggie and Braddock, and Jimmy. Son James Pitzer Gills, III, M.D.–better known as Pit Gills–is an ophthalmologist. He and his wife Joy Parker-Gills have one child, James Pitzer Gills, IV.

WELCOME TO LOVE PRESS!

Love Press is an international publishing outreach of St. Luke's Cataract & Laser Institute in Tarpon Springs, Fla., founded by James P. Gills, M.D. Because of Dr. Gills' belief in ministering not only to people's eyes, but to their whole being, St. Luke's has been giving away his inspirational books since 1985. In 1990, Dr. Gills' ministry acquired the name Love Press. His books are distributed free of charge.

Love Press has distributed more than 3 million books and pamphlets around the world. If you believe in our message and ministry, a financial gift in any amount will be greatly appreciated. You may send your correspondence, donations and requests for additional copies of Love Press books to:

Love Press
P.O. Box 5000
Tarpon Springs, FL 34688-5000

Telephone: (727) 938-2020, Ext. 2200
(800) 282-9905, Ext. 2200
Fax: (727) 372-3605

Web address: www.lovepress.com

DID YOU ENJOY THIS BOOK?

Dr. and Mrs. James P. Gills would love to hear from you! Please let them know whether *Imaginations: More Than You Think...* has had an effect in your life or in the life of your loved ones. Send your letters to:

St. Luke's Cataract & Laser Institute
P.O. Box 5000
Tarpon Springs, FL 34688-5000